PROFESSIONAL PRAISE FOR DEHMER AND THE *I-PITCH WARRIOR* MENTALITY

"Coach Dehmer is a master of the mental game. The 1-Pitch Warrior you have in your hands gives you insight into the powerful impact the mental game will have on your program and your players' lives."

—**Brian Cain**
Mental Conditioning Coach
#1 Best-Selling Author

"The 1-Pitch Warrior simplifies the mental game of baseball. This is a must-read for any coach, player, or parent. "

—**Ron Polk , Head Coach**
Mississippi State University 1976 - 1997, 2002 - 2008
Georgia University 2000 - 2001
ABCA Hall of Fame 2009

"This is some of the most impressive material I have ever seen on the mental side of the game."

—**Perry Hill, MLB Infield Coach**
Florida Marlins 2003 World Champions

"If you want to get to the next level, then you must be a 1PW. Our program is where it is today because of Coach Dehmer and the 1PW program. These are the tools to help you become a better player and to play like a champion one-pitch-at-a-time. There is no substitute for having a mentally tough team."

—**Jon Wente, Head Baseball Coach**
Central Arizona College

"The 1PW (1-Pitch Warrior) system has changed the way we think, the way we practice, the way we play, and most importantly the way we live. It helps us to focus on the journey more than just the destination; the process instead of the outcome. We are better coaches because of the use of 1PW. We even embroidered it on the back of our game caps last season so our players can remind themselves of their role every time they put it on."

—Clark Stringfellow
Bountiful High School
Head Baseball/Asst. Football
Athletic Director
Utah High School Baseball Coaches Association President

"Using the 1PW system allowed us to focus on the process and not the outcome. We spent our time working to win pitches, outs, innings, and earning our check marks rather than thinking about the end result. The kids really bought in to it and it allowed them to be in the present moment when playing the game. Being a 1PW was a difference-maker for the Clarke Indians and put us in the position to play for a state title."

—Lindsay Diehl Head Softball Coach
Clarke High School
3A Runner-Up 2013

"I will try to put into words the impact that the 1PW mentality had on our program this season.

We began establishing routines way back in October 2012, and continued throughout winter training sessions where we charted absolutely everything. We had Front Toss Scoring Systems and Barrels Charts, and constantly put players under the gun in game-like situations for them to practice their routines. Measurement truly equals Motivation. We drove home the importance of flushing our MENTAL BRICKS by having players trying to hit while holding 2-3 bats, or locate their fastballs while holding 2 baseballs. We reminded players to BREATHE in greatness, play in the present moment, AND most importantly, to play the game 1-PITCH-AT-A-TIME.

We recently captured out 1st AAA Provincial Championship this past September. Battling 200 Feet at a Time, we fought through a 12-team, double knockout tournament after losing our first game on Friday. With no margin for error, we eliminated the 3-time defending champion after trailing 4-2 and down to our last out on Saturday. We then had to knock off an undefeated team in back-to-back games on the next day to win the title. We overcame a 3-0 deficit and game #1, and were down 5-0 after 1 in game # 2. Our ATTITUDE never wavered. The boys maintained PERSPECTIVE. Their EFFORT was steadfast. I truly BELIEVE that the lessons learned in your 1PW system were in the dugout all weekend, and trust the boys will lean on their experiences when facing adversity on and off the baseball field. I know I will continue to use them myself."

—Frank Maury, Head Coach
Brampton Royals

"Coach Dehmer's 1PW System is hands down the best system out there for helping players understand what you are asking them to do in practice and games. The system takes all of the difficult-to-express, intangible things in baseball and puts them into language and processes that are simple for players to comprehend, as well as, quick and easy for coaches to implement. Not only that, but IT FLAT OUT WORKS!!! If you implement B.A.S.E.2. and the TPI into a process-versus-outcome-based coaching philosophy, you will be amazed at how accurate, and motivating to players it really is.

Instead of a player being frustrated in a game where he may go 0 for 4 but hit the ball hard twice and moved a runner into scoring position, they understand what quality ABs mean and are excited about what they did for the team. The 1PW system gives you a way to track all of the positive things that happen in a game that will never show up on the scoreboard or scorebook. I have been coaching for 20 years now and I have NEVER come across a better system. Coach Dehmer is also one of the best mental game coaches around. If you are looking for something that will instantly make a difference in your program, the 1PW system is THE system to have."

—Clay Chournos
Bear River High School
Former President Utah High School Baseball Coaches Association
2004 State Champion

"The 1PW system is everything our program needed to expand our focus on the mental game. Everything combined in the 1PW system has provided us with the ability to motivate our players by measuring both their physical and mental sides to the game. This has created confidence and results for both our players and coaches, on and off the diamond. Before finding the 1PW system, I spent days trying to combine ways to implement the mental game into our program. Now, after one season using the material in this system, I am confident that I have found the best possible way to get the much-needed mental messages across to my players. We will continue to build our program around the process of becoming a 1PW."

—Rob Wood, Head Baseball Coach
Pleasant Valley High School

"I have had the pleasure of serving our state coaches' association for over ten years as the person in charge of lining up speakers for our state clinic. I can honestly say that Coach Dehmer did an outstanding job when he spoke at our clinic. All of his presentations were very well-prepared, the topics very relevant for all high school coaches, and the concepts are easy to transfer/introduce to your team.

Last year I introduced some of his concepts to my team—collecting as much data as I could—the numbers Coach Dehmer uses in his Quality At-Bats and B.A.S.E.2. systems are dead on. It is a very useful tool in explaining the "game inside the game" to our players— making them understand that it is not about their individual batting averages, but what they can do to help our team win. This, combined with his Team Process Index and A3P, can really help your players understand what they need to do to increase their chances of winning.

Coach Dehmer also did an outstanding job in explaining some of the techniques used with his team in the mental side of the game with outstanding tips on relaxation/focus and process over results.

If you want your team to get BIG and be 1-Pitch Warriors, then reading his books and watching his DVDs are must for any coach at any level to be the best they can possibly be."

—**Mark Carroll, Head Baseball Coach**
Denham Springs High School
Executive Director
Louisiana Baseball Coaches Association

"We feel the 1-Pitch Warrior system is a great tool that helps our players reach their full potential. It will be a staple in our program for years to come."

—Carrie Embree
All-American Softball St. Thomas
Head Softball Coach Waukee High School

"This is my 30th year to coach high school baseball. I have talked to my players forever about the fact that there is more to helping our team win than their batting average. Two years ago we started tracking Coach Dehmer's QABs. Last year we talked extensively in our preseason about QABs and how this could help our team win games. Our kids really bought into it and we charted it and discussed the results with them weekly. Amazingly, stuff that we have tried to get across to our players for years suddenly made sense to them when they could see the numbers we were trying to get in each game individually and as a team! The 'game-within-the-game' that, in the long run wins for you, suddenly was a major focal point for our players. We also used several other parts of Coach Dehmer's system, including the TPI and the 'first three pitches chart.' I had the pleasure of hearing Coach Dehmer speak at our state coaching clinic and really got an indepth view to his system—I will listen to anybody who put together a winning streak like the one he did. I strongly suggest that you try this system with your team—I guarantee you will see a positive influence on your players as they get a deeper understanding of what it takes to win games!

—Mark Carro
Denham Springs High School

"Being in the moment, playing the game 1-pitch-at-a-time, is the perfect formula for a player's success. The more our players buy into Coach Dehmer's 1-Pitch Warrior principles, the better they are able to perform. Our 2011 and 2013 State Championship teams are perfect examples of dealing with the adversities of the game and finding success through the process-oriented 1-Pitch Warrior system. If you're not implementing something to improve the mental game, you are selling your players short. Coach Dehmer's 1-Pitch Warrior approach will help your players find success."

—*Joey Sato, Head Baseball Coach*
Bingham High School
5A State Champions 1999, 2003, 2011, 2013

101 TOOLS

EQUIPPED FOR

EXCELLENCE

JUSTIN B. DEHMER
1-Pitch Warrior, LLC

Visit www.1pitchwarrior.com/free
for the BONUS *1-Pitch Warrior*
9 "Innings" of Free Training Resources!

www.1pitchwarrior.com
Twitter: @1pitchwarrior
www.facebook.com/1pitchwarrior

Justin B. Dehmer
1-Pitch Warrior: 101 Tools—Equipped for Excellence
A 1-Pitch Warrior Series Book
1-Pitch Warrior Publishing
1-Pitch Warrior, LLC
©2013 by Justin Dehmer, All Rights Reserved.

Brian Cain has generously given permission to include tools, tips, and ideas from his copyrighted works: Toilets, Bricks, Fish Hooks, and PRIDE, So What, Next Pitch!, and The Mental Conditioning Manual

Printed in the United States of America
Edited by: Cristine Hammer
Cover Design and Layout: David Brizendine
Illustrations: Justin Dehmer
Photography: Flash Digital Photography

ISBN: 978-0-9912109-0-9

PREFACE

1-*Pitch Warrior: 101 Tools—Equipped for Excellence* is intended to give you ideas to run with—ways to make your program better and better until you reach excellence. Some things you may already do so I hope that the concepts and techniques reinforce what you are currently doing. In other cases, the chapters may give you ways to do the same old thing you have done for years but in a new way. The challenge is to find new ways to create growth in the way you operate your program to provide the best learning experience for your players. Whenever I attend a clinic, I always try to walk away with two to three ideas that spark something new for me to build off of. My hope is that you are able to find more than two or three ideas within the 101 Chapters of what it takes to be a *1-Pitch Warrior*. The topics in the book range from ways to measure the process both at practice and in games, mental game ideas, practice organization, program builders, team builders, my favorite drills/teaching tools, and charting. I am confident that you will learn much and will be able to apply the concepts to your program immediately. The best coaches never stop learning and searching for better ways. I applaud you for your passion and determination for growth and on becoming a *1-Pitch Warrior*.

DEDICATION

This book is dedicated to the two biggest gifts life has given me—my kids, Grace and Gavin. May you chase your dreams and know that anything is possible. Your grandparents provided me with a compass and with unconditional support. Now it is my turn. I will be there to celebrate your joys and, when life gets tough, to help you play the next pitch.

Your biggest fan,

Love Dad

ACKNOWLEDGMENTS

W.O.W.! I am honored and humbled before God to live my purpose to honor Him and help other coaches pursue excellence through the grace that He provides. God is the ultimate *1-Pitch Warrior* and none of what I do or have done would be possible without His love. I could not have imagined what the *1-Pitch Warrior* Mentality would grow into thanks to His blessing.

I have been fortunate beyond belief in all areas of my life. To have the support of great friends and family is something I am truly grateful for. Thank you for your support in my decision to resign as a head coach and invest more time with my kids. Also, through some difficult times over the past years, you have been there to help me stay focused on taking it one-thing-at-a-time. I love you all. You know who you are.

Special thanks to Jon Fitzpatrick for being the best friend a guy could ever ask for. To John and JoAnn Dehmer for being the best parents I could have asked for. And thanks to Brian Cain for spurring me on to create something of significance to share with others and for being a continuing mentor.

Big thanks to all the coaches, players, and parents who believe in the *1-Pitch Warrior* Mentality, have adopted it in their programs, and live it every day. Continue to focus on the process, win pitches in the present, and win your days as a *1-Pitch Warrior*!

If you have a dream or a goal—Go all in! No holding back! You must ACT BIG, BREATHE BIG, and COMMIT BIG!

CONTENTS

1-Pitch Warrior Process-Based Measurement System

Practice Data Measurement

Ideas to Build Your Program

Ways to Build Team Unity

Favorite Drills and Teaching Aids

Other Charting

FORWARD

Like most everyone reading this, I have been around baseball for my entire life. My dad took me to the ball field four or five times a week, to professional baseball games every year, and always worked on my skills. I caught in high school and in college, so I felt like I knew how to develop a pitcher from the beginning of the year, to game day and throughout the season, and how to manage a pitcher throughout a game. I always enjoyed picking the brains of others around me about everything baseball. Plus, I had even coached high school baseball the previous summer back home and had a great experience doing so. In 2009, I just graduated college, finished my college baseball career, and completed my student teaching. I was 21-years-old and thought I knew a lot, especially about baseball.

In the spring semester of my senior year, I mentioned something to one of my baseball coaches about wanting to coach baseball in the summer and eventually become a head coach some day. He told me about an assistant coaching position at Martensdale-St. Marys. Not growing up in central Iowa, I knew absolutely nothing about Martensdale-St. Marys Baseball or the community. So, I decided to apply for the position and got an interview. At the interview, Coach Dehmer asked all of the typical interview questions and then filled me in on the history behind Martensdale-St. Marys Baseball. The program had won a state championship in 2004 and only had one losing season in the last 30 years. Needless to say, the expectations were very high. However, I will always remember what Coach Dehmer said next. "Our goal is to win a state championship, but in order to do this, we have to take care of a lot of little things along the way." I just smiled and nodded, thinking how nice it would be to actually win a state championship. Little did I know, this is exactly how we would operate the program for the next few years. Even though it took me a while before I clearly understood what he meant, looking back on it, Coach Dehmer was talking about focusing on the process and not worrying about the outcome.

After accepting the position as Coach Dehmer's assistant, he invited me over to his home to talk about his coaching philosophy and how he runs the program. I was thinking we would look at practice plans and talk about different hitting drills to help improve our athletes' skills. However, after talking with Justin for less than five minutes, I knew there was something different about him as a coach and an individual. His attention to detail was like nothing I had ever seen before. When he started talking about the mental game, I could relate to most of what he was talking about, but it was a foreign language to me. Neither my high school coach nor any of my college coaches ever talked about the mental game. It was like I was back sitting in my college Physics class, with all of the information just going over my head. It is pretty safe to say my head was spinning. And then, Justin pulled out all of the charts he uses to help keep track of the players' progress throughout the year. We talked about Quality At-Bats, B.A.S.E.2., and Quality Innings, among others. I had never seen a coach more organized and focused on what really matters in baseball. Like I said, I have been around baseball my entire life and I honestly think I learned more about the mental side of baseball in the three hours we talked than I had in 21 years.

After I spent the day with Coach Dehmer and learned a little about the mental game and the true process of baseball, I still was curious about how this was all going to be implemented and how you could possibly fit all of this mental game work into a practice. However, after just one day, I had no doubt we could win a state championship, and this was before I had even met the players. After our first official practice in May, I could see the pieces falling into place. We started practice with a "skull session," which was a quick but much-focused talk on the mental game for the day. When live hitting took place, we kept track of quality at-bats and played each at-bat live. I had never been around this kind of atmosphere and I absolutely loved it. Every drill we did had a focus and purpose. The best part was the players knew why we did every drill and how it was making them better.

My first year I really just tried soaking up as much information was I possibly could. Even though I had been a high school coach before I soon realized if you are not seeking out new information and knowledge you will never get better. The 2009 season finished without that trip to the state tournament. The varsity team finished 25-11 and started only one senior. However, what really had me excited was our JV team was 23-2. I knew with Coach Dehmer's philosophy and the talent we had coming back, we would make it to Principal Park (host to Iowa's State Tournament). In 2010 we had a magical run. The JV finished the season 23-1 and the varsity team became only the ninth team in Iowa High School Baseball history to go unbeaten, finishing with a record of 43-0. There is no doubt in my mind Coach Dehmer's *1-Pitch Warrior* philosophy and the players buying into the mental game led us to this unthinkable record.

After the 2010 season I interviewed for a head coaching position. I initially interviewed for the experience of going through an interview for a head coaching position. After just completing an unbeaten season and returning many key components, I had repeat on my mind. After going through the interview and hearing what the school had to say, I started thinking about maybe taking the head coaching position. As you can imagine, this was not an easy decision. How could I possibly leave this juggernaut of a program? How could I step away from the possibility of another state championship? Most of all, how could I leave Coach Dehmer after everything he had taught me? After going back and forth many times, I decided to take the head coaching position. Deep down I knew if I implemented the *1-Pitch Warrior* mentality and introduced the mental game to this new program, I would be able to turn the program around.

I remember the first night I met with the parents and players at my new school. I talked about the mental game and my expectations for the season. I had set the bar rather high for a team coming off a below .500 season. But after this first meeting, I had many parents come up to me and tell me how excited they were to see the discipline and high expectations upfront. When we had our first off-season throwing session, I started introducing the mental game little by little. At first the guys just kind of had a blank stare on their faces. They didn't really know what to think. But I stuck with it and kept talking about the mental game and knew it would work. We finished 2011 with a 24-8 record and set many school records. We had our ups and downs, but the framework of the mental game was definitely in place. The players bought in from day one and I knew the second season was going to be much easier to implement. We returned a solid group in 2012 and the expectations were pretty high. I knew we would have to rely on the mental game even more throughout the season. The best part of the 2012 season was seeing the guys really put the mental game into action – seeing pitchers and hitters taking a deep breath before each pitch, seeing guys "flush" their last at-bat with routines we had created, and hearing the common language the team had developed with terms like "So What Next Pitch" and "Flush It." One of my favorite memories as a coach was when my best player slid into 3rd after a huge triple that knocked the starting pitcher out of the game. While the opposing coach was making the pitching change, my player looked at me and said, "You know, Coach, this mental game stuff really works. At the beginning of last year I was a young punk who thought he was better than everyone else. Now, I know how to play the game the right way." This still gives me chills because it shows just how powerful the mental game can be. We finished the 2012 season with a 34-9 overall record and won the first outright conference championship ever.

After the 2012 season, Coach Dehmer decided to step down as the head coach at Martensdale-St. Marys. I applied for the head coaching position and got the job. Everyone I talked to about the position said the same thing, "Who would want to replace Coach Dehmer?" I completely understood what they were talking about considering he just led Martensdale-St. Marys to three straight 1A state championships, including an 88-game win streak. However, I knew I learned everything from the best and taking over his program was an honor for me. Even when I was not coaching with Justin for two years, I still talked to him on a daily basis, just picking his brain and gaining valuable advice.

I am very blessed to have met Justin. Not only is he one of the best coaches, but he is an even better individual. I learned so much from him about coaching and about life. The best part about the *1-Pitch Warrior* mentality is it translates to everyday life. Everyone will have their ups and downs in school, work, and relationships, but having a process to get through it makes a huge difference. The one piece of advice I have for coaches in implementing the *1-Pitch Warrior* program is that it is an every day thing, not a once-in-a-while thing. Like I mentioned earlier, when I got my first head coaching job, it took a year to build the framework. By the second year, I was able to build around the framework I already created and it only got better from there. I now have two mottos I remember, not only when coaching, but also in everyday life—1. Do a little a lot, not a lot of little, and 2. Today + Today + Today = Season = Career. If you start talking about the mental game every day and make it a part of your program, you will see the benefits over time.

–Jon Fitzpatrick
Head Baseball Coach
Martensdale-St. Marys

INTRODUCTION

Eighty-Eight wins in a row. To this day, I have a hard time believing that we actually won that many consecutive games. Despite all the variables innate to baseball on a nightly basis—an opposing pitcher who is lights out on the mound, defensive miscues, mental mistakes, bats that have gone cold, coaching mistakes, or any number of other factors that come with coaching high school players and the subtleties of baseball— we were able to overcome all of these things for 88 straight games and win three straight state titles from 2010 to 2012, too. You will hear me say time and time again, that we were not perfect... ever. It is plain that we do not preach perfection in our program; what we do preach is knowing that adversity will come our way in many forms throughout the season and that, no matter what the situation, we must be able to handle it and yet still strive for excellence in all we do. In every game, there was good and bad. What we did better than our opponents was not only prepare for success, but also plan for failure. We played the game as *1-Pitch Warriors*, which became our motto throughout our winning streak. Even after it was over, it transitioned into my business and passion to spread that culture and mentality to as many baseball and softball programs as possible.

As we continued our streak from 43 wins in a row in 2010, to 44 more consecutive wins in 2011, and 1 more in 2012, it became very clear to me that this phenomenon was much more about the way we prepared for each night than simply having great players. There is no doubt that we were a very talented team and that talent does not hurt when it comes to winning games. But talent alone does not, and never will, mean certain victory. To win 88 times in a row, through three consecutive state titles, with a schedule that demanded focus night in and night out, had to be the result of much more than just physical skill and luck. We played almost every night, starting the last week of May and continuing through the 4th of July week until the postseason started in the second week of July. We prepared relentlessly on the field—hitting, fielding, throwing, pitching, running the bases, etc. All the fundamentals were covered, but what I feel took us to the next level and allowed for the wins and titles was our mental approach to the game. During the 2010, 2011, and 2012 seasons, we became *1-Pitch Warriors* and my players will always have that mentality as long as I coach. I feel it is the only way to play the game with consistency and to play your best when you need it most.

1-Pitch Warrior: 101 Tools—Equipped for Excellence is the behind-the-scenes access to that unrelenting focus on getting better every day, which allowed us to reach greatness. Whether it is my favorite drills to incorporate into your next practice, or how to win the game-inside-a-game with systems like B.A.S.E.2., TPI, QABs, A3P, S.T.R.1.K.E.; whether you are a veteran or rookie coach, there is something in here for everyone. It takes into account all aspects of coaching from the mental game, to the planning, measuring your progress, and much more. Keeping focused on the process, winning pitches in the present, and dominating your days is the *1-Pitch Warrior* Mentality.

Special Thanks to Brian Cain

I want to take this opportunity to thank Brian Cain for his many innovative ways in approaching the games of baseball, softball, and more importantly, life. I know that the lessons I learned from him are game changers, on and off the field. Not only have they helped in our team's most successful moments, but they have also helped me personally through some very tough times.

He has forever changed the way I coach by instilling the concept that it is not about the outcome but only the things you can control. I want to extend my gratitude to him for allowing me to get to know him both professionally and personally. I set out to write a book about how I coached during our streak of 88 consecutive wins and back-to-back-to-back state titles at Martensdale-St. Marys. There is no doubt the influence Brian had on it and on this book, too. I am very appreciative and humbled that he would be gracious enough to allow me to share with you many of his concepts and ideas that I incorporated into our coaching. You will find that many of the mental game ideas presented in this book, along with others tools, are adapted straight from his teachings.

Brian inspired me to think in new ways and to know that greatness is only one pitch away. He was the driving force behind my first book and I thank him for allowing the second to happen in a way that gives you total access to all the strategies I used as a coach. I hope these 101 Tools impact your program empowering you to achieve excellence!

1-PITCH WARRIOR PROCESS-BASED MEASUREMENT SYSTEM

Measurement = Motivation
Measure what you treasure.
Be about the PROCESS

Player Process Index – PPI

I firmly believe, that in any area of life, the path to success is determined by the actions you take and there are specific steps that you can take to make your journey to the top a quicker one. I have learned from others that success leaves clues. By trade I am a math teacher so the statistical side of things just makes sense for me to use, but also I feel it helps give players a better way to view the game, knowing that there are certain things that they can do correctly—committing to the process—to help them have the desired outcome. I want our players to focus on the things that they can control (The Process) and not the end result.

Let's face it. The way baseball statistics are calculated is an unfair way to do things. Hitters typically judge themselves on their average, which to me is a terrible way for players to view their performances. A pitcher could hit a screaming line drive to the shortstop, ground out to the 2nd baseman to advance a runner from 2nd base to 3rd base, and grind out a very long at-bat, before getting an out, ultimately wearing that pitcher down during a turning point in the game. The newspaper the next day would show that this player is 0 for 3, with no RBIs, and according to the old way of thinking did nothing productive that day, which is entirely wrong. I will discuss in detail later how using a Quality At-Bat Average is a much better way to view plate appearances than your traditional batting average, or even on-base percentage.

Pitchers typically look at their win/loss record to determine whether they are having a good season. Again, this is a very unfair way to tell if they are actually playing well. There are far too many things that go into losing a game to give sole credit to your starting pitcher or reliever for "losing" the game, but quite often it are the pitchers that carry the load of the loss squarely on their shoulders. Later, I will also touch on many pitcher statistics that are grounded in the process of things they can control and not on what may be going on around them. Many times pitchers are responsible, or play a major part in the loss, but other times they are not. The statistics I will teach you will help you get a true sense of performance and assess the areas that lead to giving your team the best chance to win games.

With the *1-Pitch Warrior* Statistical Player Process Index (PPI), we can provide players with much more meaningful data on how they are really performing and also give them areas they can grow in. The statistics we use are ones that we are able to replicate during practice, which also makes it great for players to understand that this is not just a game thing. The statistics I am going to teach you are all process-based—things that the players can control. We want the players to focus on things that they can control, because "getting at hit" is not an attainable goal for an at-bat, while hitting a ball hard is. Striking a guy out is not an attainable goal, while having a plan to hit spots/throw strikes is. I tell players that once the ball leaves your bat and once the ball leaves your hand on the mound, the outcome is quite literally out of your hands. Players must learn to accept this as a fact. That is why dealing in the process and not the outcome is just a better way to play the game.

After keeping years and years of data, we can conclude what things we must do to give ourselves the best chance of success during the course of a game. I will give you the benchmarks for each category so you and your players have something to strive for. These benchmarks are not just from my teams. Across the country, many coaches who already use the *1-Pitch Warrior* System have told me that they are finding the percentages to be rock solid!

1. QUALITY AT-BATS (QAB)

Most coaches can agree that the game of baseball is an unfair game. I think Augie Garrido said it best when he said that players are playing against two things: 1) themselves and 2) the game. Let's explore these more in depth. Hitting a round ball with a round bat is quite possibly the toughest thing to do in sports. Many players base their feelings on how things are going during the season based on statistics—mainly, what is their batting average. If they are 0 for 4, they had a rough night, their average drops, and their confidence typically does the same thing. But, there is a problem with the way averages are calculated because they are influenced by some things that are beyond a hitter's control. A player who squares up to a ball, hits it hard, but a fielder makes an amazing play, should get credit for doing what he set out to do—hit the ball hard or have a productive team at-bat. The concept we need to get our players to understand is that it is much more than just getting a hit. Just getting a hit is a terrible way for players to judge their contributions to the team. But unfortunately, this is what they see every night on ESPN and the MLB Network. It is a tough barrier to break down, but one that is worth it. I feel there is a fundamental flaw with the way averages work because it robs players of times they do all they can, but have nothing to show for it. In my mind it may be the worst single statistic in all of sports.

For example, what if a hitter goes 0 for 3 on the night and the at-bats go like this:

1. Line out to 3rd base

2. Lays a bunt down to move runners to 3rd and 2nd

3. Scores a run from 3rd with less than 2 outs by weakly grounding out to the middle infield that was playing back

4. Grinds out a long 9-pitch at-bat by fouling off pitch after pitch late in the game, which ultimately leads to the opposing team going to the bullpen

Did this player have a terrible night? He did go 0 for 3. The game summary will clearly read that way the following day. When people pick up the paper the next day, it will look as if Johnny Ballplayer's only contribution was the RBI. Will this player be able to see past the zero he put up in the hits column? Do you currently have a system in place that is both process-oriented and team-based to combat this hitter's "terrible" night?

If you do not, then you are running the risk of this player going home that night making up his own mind about how things went. In my opinion, I feel this player has every right to leave the diamond feeling great about the way he played for his team. In my mind and the *1-Pitch Warrior* Quality At-Bat System, he did go 4 for 4. Traditional scorekeeping says that the player was 0 for 3, but by giving the player a different lens through which to view his performance, he actually had a great night and his QAB% was 100%. Using a QAB % changes a player's entire perspective on the game he has played for years. Most players are only worried about one thing—getting hits—which is not a bad thing, but I want players to evaluate themselves differently with QABs. I know the scenario I created may seem like a bit of a stretch. But how many times have you had a player line out two straight plate appearances and then start swinging harder or trying to do too much at the dish, when what he is already doing is working. He just is not happy with the results. Before long, he is in a slump trying to get hits, when getting a hit is out of his control. All he can control is squaring up to the ball. QABs help players evaluate themselves and can keep them from getting wrapped up in the traditional approach to calculating outcome as a hitter.

If you have read any of Brian Cain's books or *Head's Up Baseball*, you know the fundamental of the mental game of baseball/ softball that players must learn to accept as a fact is that they have very little control of what goes around them in the game, including whether or not they get hits. They do not control that. They can only control if they hit the ball hard. In this system, they get credit for productive at-bats/process-oriented outs.

The idea of a QAB is not something new to the game. Teams from all over have players coming back into dugouts, congratulating each other for their quality at-bats. Coaches talk about having quality at-bats all the time. But, have you ever created a structured plan for what a quality at-bat actual is? If you asked the players in your program to define what a QAB is, what would they say?

You have to instruct what QBAs are and teach your players how they will be evaluated on a QAB% rather than their average.

Start to calculate QABs for players during games and especially during practice. I am a firm believer that if I am going to measure a player a certain way during a game, then I should also measure that same thing during practice. If that cannot happen then it probably is not a reliable statistic to keep. My coaching philosophy and methods are influenced by keeping and determining the ways data can better serve us as coaches and players.

In the *1PW* System, there are 9 things that a player can do to get credit for QAB:

1. Hard Hit Ball

2. Walk

3. Hit by Pitch

4. Move Runner(s) with No Outs

5. Score Runner from 3rd with Fewer Than Two Outs

6. Base Hit

7. Six Pitches At-Bat Not Ending in a Strikeout

8. Nine Pitches At-Bat Even Ending in a Strikeout

9. Catcher's Interference

The list of 9 QABs is very straightforward. The only one that is questionable at times is whether the ball was hard hit. Coaches, you will have the ultimate say in that. But, if your players start asking you, know they have "bought in." Other programs may have a variation of the 9 QABs, but the aforementioned list is what we have used. The point is to have some measures as a set list of criteria used to evaluate rather than some philosophy or concept players cannot understand. To me, it is a no-brainer to show a player a QAB Average as opposed to his "traditional" average. What I have found typically is you can expect a player's QAB Average to be two times higher than his traditional average. Would you rather show a player that he is hitting .300 or .600? Which number will the player feel better about? Which is more team-oriented?

The QAB System means that every plate appearance counts. No 0 for 0 for a walk or sacrifice. Everything counts and means something. I believe the QAB System is one of the reasons we have been able to draw huge amounts of walks over the past three years, which has also led to us scoring more runs. Again, players are not at the plate trying to get a hit, because they know that with the perspective shift within our program, even grinding out a long at-bat can still result in a QAB and a walk is a QAB, too.

The numbers that follow are our three seasons leading up to our state championships. These numbers show how many walks we were drawing, which certainly increases the number of runs we score by creating more base runners, and also wears the starting pitchers down by having them throw strikes. Call me crazy, but I would rather a player have a 7-pitch at-bat and walk, than go up and hit one hard on the first or second pitch. We want to get to the bullpen as early as possible and the best way to accomplish that is to be patient and have plate discipline. When you start to measure what you want, your players will buy into that philosophy. Measure what you treasure.

The Numbers:

2010 — 222 Walks, 459 Runs

2011 — 210 Walks, 445 Runs

2012 — 229 Walks, 474 Runs

Total — 661 Walks, 1378 Runs

In these three seasons we were second, fourth, and second respectively in the state at drawing the walk. I do believe it is in large part due to the QAB System we implemented. Offensively, I feel there is no other way to evaluate oneself as an individual in a way that is team-based, process-oriented, and fair for players.

Why is QAB Percentage Useful?

If you were a track coach trying to make the lineup for the 4x4 relay, how would you decide which runner to use for that event? This is a no-brainer and laughable. We all know the fastest runners are the ones who will be part of the event. For years, Baseball and Softball have used a more subjective approach to making out the lineup. Using a QAB percentage is to a head baseball/softball coach what a stopwatch is to a track coach. Using the system makes things much more black and white.

As a coach, this is how I approach using the statistic of QAB Percentage. I teach our incoming freshman about it and remind those who are already apart of our program that this is the best way to get into the lineup. I tell them that I do not look at their averages; I do not care what they are. What I do care about is how high your QAB% is. For the first three weeks of practice during our situational hitting portion of practice, we measure the players' plate appearances on the same criteria we use to evaluate them in the game. This is when players start to buy into the system and really start to understand it. They will start lobbying for a hard hit ball for their teammates or know they had a 6-pitch at-bat. It is awesome to see.

We keep track of all of this and, after each week of practice is over, we post the results so players can start to see where they stack up against each other. They know that it is going to be hard to crack the lineup if they do not have one of the top 9 or 10 highest QAB averages. What a powerful tool for a coach to have at his disposal. No more guessing on who is doing better, or who we "think" performed better at practice leading up to the big game. Players also know you are recording it and it makes practices that much more pressure-packed. They know they are competing against the guy next to them and it is not coach's opinion that counts or who he likes more that will determine whose name is on the lineup card. If, throughout the regular season, we were platooning a couple of players at a certain position, keeping track their QAB average would help me make that decision on whom I might go with for our post-season push. I can sit both players down together and show them where each one is at and show them the better starter for our first playoff game because that player has a higher QAB percentage. I have done this every year and never had any problems because players can understand it and accept it as a fact. It is not filled with emotion. It is a very objective way to coach and fair for all.

During the season, as we record the data, we continue to show the players on bus rides or post results in our dugout. Another important thing to note is that our coaches never do the QAB Chart. One of our players will always be responsible for it. You will have to teach them how to do it, but that only takes about 5 minutes. I feel this keeps players in the game with a chance to learn the system even better.

This is something that could be used as ammo for the parent

who really thinks his or her kid should be in the lineup but is not. They are going to tell you how much better their son/daughter is than so and so. You can show them that you have based your decision over the course of the season and that their son's or daughter's QAB% is not as high as others. Most of the time that will end the conversation.

Benchmark

As I told you, after years of doing this I have come to a statistical benchmark to aim for during the game. I call it the "game-within-a-game." I have found that in our program, both on JV and Varsity, when we get to 60%, we win a majority of the time. Many coaches who have adopted the QAB philosophy and made the commitment to follow through have found similar results.

The breakdown:

When at or above 60%, our JV/Varsity has been 269-12-4.

When below 60%, our JV/Varsity has been 59-43-6.

Use the 60% benchmark to guide the way you handle your players in talking about changes and use this breakdown to determine when you should intervene with a player's swing mechanics, mental approach, etc.

- **GO!** – 70% or above on QABs and no adjustments are needed at this point. If it's not broke, don't fix it.

- **WHOA!** – 60% to 69% is a great place to be and slight changes could produce better results, but even those may need to be considered carefully.

- **SO, SO** – 50% to 59% leaves room for improvement and might be a kid struggling to crack the lineup. Physically and mentally, players need to make changes. Investigate ways to improve.

- **OH NO!!** – Below 50% is a cause for concern and a definite eye opener for both the coach and the player. We want to keep working on making solid contact and good pitch selection, along with a physical plan in place to fix mechanical flaws and a sound routine to focus on 1-pitch-at-a-time at the plate.

It is a great topic to talk about with your team after games to drive home the point of how important having those QABs really are. Keep track and set team records for individual games, seasons, and individual season records. We even go so far at the end of the year to award a Quality At-Bat Champion on both JV and Varsity. In other words keep the main thing, the main thing. QAB and B.A.S.E.2., which I will discuss next, are the only two offensive philosophies we stick to. I do not want to make it too complicated.

2. B.A.S.E.2.

The only other offensive statistic we keep is the B.A.S.E.2. philosophy. Quality At-Bats are how we measure our players' individual performances and B.A.S.E.2. is how we measure our team's overall offensive performance. As I have already mentioned, I believe in working the process. Through that process will we find the results we want, if are able to complete a few specific tasks. Get three of the five parts of B.A.S.E.2. and the winning will take care of itself.

What B.A.S.E.2. does is put an emphasis on *how* you score runs, instead of *just* scoring runs in some random fashion. We all understand that scoring runs is the name of the game, but

B.A.S.E.2. puts a premium on how those runs need to be scored and may change your coaching philosophy in the process. The following is a description of each criterion that your team needs to complete to earn credit for that portion of B.A.S.E.2.

Big Inning

Your team would earn credit for a big inning if they were able to score three or more runs during the course of the game. This can happen in the first inning, or it can happen in the fifth. It does not matter when, only that it occurs at least once. Your team would not earn multiple credits for doing it again at a later inning in the game. If your team scores one run every inning, you may put up some runs, but a big inning was not recorded and statistics show that the team with the biggest inning in the course of a game typically wins the game.

Answer Back

This may be my favorite aspect of the B.A.S.E.2. Philosophy. An example of earning credit for the Answer Back portion would be the other team scores two runs in the bottom half of the third inning. Your team comes back in and scores in the top half of the fourth inning. An extreme example would be that the other team scores 12 runs in the top half of the second inning and your team comes to bat and scores one run. As you can see, the number of runs either team scores is not the point. The point is to put up a fight and not lay down. Take your shots, but keep getting back up. We are trying to kill even a little of the other team's momentum by Answering Back. Again, this is not something that you can earn more than once. If you answer back again later in the game, you do not double up on this. Remember, measurement equals motivation so once you start recording how well you are doing using B.A.S.E.2., your players will begin to understand how important it is to score after they may have given up a few runs. You will know once they have bought into the System because they will come back into the dugout yelling to each other, "Let's Answer Back!" It guides your team on how you want to play the game.

Score First

This one should be self-explanatory, but I think it deserves a bit of attention on how you might approach the first few at-bats your team has. Obviously, only one team can score first. Once this chance is gone, there is no opportunity to earn it back at a later point in the game. So, if you are home and the visitors score in the top half of the first inning, you have lost out on the "S" in B.A.S.E.2. The best you would be able to do is Answer Back in the bottom half. This is one reason I actually like being the visitors and, during tournaments or coin flips, to see who would be home or away. It is not uncommon for me to pick visitors, or be really happy when the other team picks home. This way, our team always has the opportunity to get credit for scoring first without having to put up a shutout first inning on defense. Our team started to adopt that philosophy, as well, because they knew that we are going to try to come out in the first and score at least one run, at any cost.

This is where I think my coaching philosophy may have changed over the years. Early on in my coaching career, I think I saved the bunt game for later in the game and tried to drive runs in with hits early in the game. After using the B.A.S.E.2. System and understanding and realizing the importance of scoring first, it does not matter to me how that first run comes across, but I spare no expense to get it in if that means bunting any one of my hitters. If the other team already scored first and stole it away from us, then my coaching style changed a bit on how I try to score runs.

Extend the Lead

The fourth criteria you are trying to achieve is to extend the lead. This is a great way to play through an entire game. We have all been in the situation where the first four or five innings go great, we have a sizeable lead, and then we just coast for the rest of the game. I am sure there is a game you can think of immediately when you gave up a W because you got lackadaisical and the other team rallied to score. Say the game is tied and we have a big inning in the fourth. We score six runs to put us up in the game. I want to continue putting pressure on the other team— either finish them off with the run-rule, or at least add some insurance runs. Extending the lead must occur in two separate innings—not the same inning. In my previous example, we went up six runs. If we score the next inning, we earn the extend-the-lead opportunity. It does not have to happen in subsequent innings, either. If you score two runs in the first and hold the other team scoreless, then you score again in the sixth inning, you have extended the lead. I need to mention that you can only get credit for extending the lead once, like the other criteria. Even if you continue to extend the lead in multiple innings, you do not get extra credit for them.

Score with 2 Outs

The last thing our offense is trying to accomplish is to score with two outs. This seems like a simple idea, but there are some areas of gray. Just to eliminate the gray areas, the way I have always done this is, if we score with two outs we earn credit for the "2." No matter if that run we scored with 2 outs, came on an error, wild pitch, hit, or any other circumstance, we earn the credit. Some coaches like to make it only an RBI with 2 outs. It is up to you. I just figured we have done enough to put ourselves in a position to score that run somehow so, if we do, we get credit. Even if the other team makes a mistake, we will take advantage. No matter how the run is scored, it is always a knock to your team when you are on defense, so close to ending the inning to come up short. It changes the momentum. Just like answering back is a momentum killer, scoring with two outs is a great way to gain some momentum on your side.

I know the B.A.S.E.2. System will be a game changer for you and your program. I cannot watch any level of baseball or softball without evaluating the game through the lens of B.A.S.E.2. It will give a way to score runs in a systematic fashion to increase your chance of winning.

Benchmark

Over the years here is what I have found, and the results are staggering. Keep in mind, we run this same system and keep track of B.A.S.E.2. for JV and Varsity. When we recorded three or more of the different facets of B.A.S.E.2., we were 259-8-2. Coaches email me, tweet me, and Facebook me all the time telling me about the same results in both baseball and softball. You can increase your chances of winning by executing at least three of the tasks. For 96.3% of the time, we won the game when we had three or more. It is astounding that there are actually teams out there not playing the game this way. Do not be one of them. You know your players have bought into the B.A.S.E.2. System once a game is over and they say, "Coach, we only had 4 checkmarks tonight when the score was 7 to 0." They will make jokes about earning the checkmarks for B.A.S.E.2., because, if they do not give up a run and shut out the other team, they will never have the opportunity to Answer Back.

Visit www.1pitchwarrior.com/free
for BONUS *1-Pitch Warrior* Tips
& FREE Systems of Success

If you are interested in the data collecting charts, the data recording spreadsheets, or any of the other PPI Systems of Success found in the *1-Pitch Warrior* System, go to www.1pitchwarrior.com to purchase the *1-Pitch Warrior: Mental Toughness Training System* DVD and my first book *1-Pitch Warrior: Mental Toughness Training System.*

Player Process Index For Pitchers

In the next section I am going to share with you some statistics that hold your pitchers accountable to what they can control. We want them to become comfortable with the fact that wins and losses are things that are out of their full control. Committing to the following processes is a much better way for our players to understand the game, improve, and realize that our chance of victory takes place when we are able to reach certain benchmarks within the PPI Statistics.

3. FIRST-PITCH STRIKE PERCENTAGE/A3P (AFTER THREE PITCHES)

Two big things we stress to pitchers are the ability to get ahead in the count and pitch to contact early. Striking guys out on seven or eight pitches is not a way to be an effective pitcher. It does not create longevity in a start and will get pitch count up quickly. We try to keep our starter in the game as long as possible—to go the distance.

Charting the first pitch strike percentage is not a revolutionary idea and most teams understand the impact of getting the first pitch for a strike can have on the rest of the at-bat, but how many teams out there are taking the time to record it? It is something simple that it is easy to do and a great way to give feedback to your pitchers on how effective they are at getting ahead.

Benchmark

We look to see if the pitcher (starter or reliever) has been at 60% on their first pitch. We found that this seems to be the magic number when it comes to first-pitch strike percentage. One thing I look for is how closely a pitcher's first-pitch strike percentage is to his overall strike percentage. I look for consistency between the two. We do not want one being ten percent higher than the other. Especially if the first-pitch strike percentage is lower than the overall, it may be a sign of poor preparation toward each new hitter. Your pitcher may have an inability to refocus on a new hitter. I am always comparing them together and letting the numbers dictate conversations I may have with that pitcher. When they are not the same, one question I usually ask them, "Is it any harder to throw a first-pitch strike than it is a strike later on in the count?" The obvious answer is no. But, sometimes the process-based measurement lets us key in on inadequacies or deficiencies in a pitcher's performance. This provides critical feedback to him, allowing for an opportunity to grow. After the game is over, we take a look with the starter and any other pitchers who threw that game. We review the statistics for the game and, if their first-pitch strike percentage was at or over 60%, then that is a plus for them. Regardless of outcome, we want the pitcher to be concerned with process and be comfortable with the loss, if statistically, he did well that night with the things he could control. If their PPI stats were low and not up to par, then they can own the loss or take a majority of the blame. It works both ways, but by keeping the statistics you can avoid the situation of a pitcher who pitched well, blame himself entirely for a loss.

A3P (After Three Pitches)

A3P is another tool we use to measure our pitchers that goes well with first-pitch strikes. What we are measuring is our pitchers' abilities to get the ball in play and get ahead in the count. Obviously, we want to get as many first-pitch strikes as possible, but an A3P can still be earned even if they do not get a first-pitch strike across. I like this approach. It is still the game-within-the-game and no letdown occurs just because the first one did not get over. An A3P is awarded in two cases:

1. The pitcher has the ball put in play within the first three pitches, regardless of outcome.

2. Gets ahead and has thrown two strikes within the first pitches.

Examples of each: A pitcher throws a ball, then another ball, and then the batter gets a double. He would earn an A3P. Remember, we are not concerned with the result when measuring the process. We are trying to keep pitch count low.

If a pitcher throws a ball, then comes back with two strikes to get back ahead, he earns an A3P.

Benchmark

What we are trying to achieve is our pitchers going through the entire order and earning at least six A3Ps. This amounts to a 66.6% overall A3P average. We have found longevity in our starters and quality outings, time and time again, when they reach this mark. Our best pitchers have always been the ones who have the highest A3P.

4. OVERALL STRIKE PERCENTAGE

Just like first-pitch strike percentage, we are recording the pitchers' overall strike percentage. As the game goes on, we record each inning for all of these. It helps me see trends also as the game goes. I am able to see if the current pitcher is getting stronger as the game proceeds, staying the same, or getting worse in terms of first pitch and overall strike percentage. It is nice to stay ahead of the curve about when, or when not, to take a pitcher out. I usually use the PPI Stats to help guide me on when to take a guy out and err on the side of doing it too early rather than too late. Every coach has been there when they second-guess the decision on whether the pitcher should have been taken out a batter earlier. The Player Process Indexes are not just for players to focus on the process; I feel they are also helpful for coaches to make informed decisions based on what has actually happened during the course of the game.

Benchmark

We look at overall strike percentage the same way we do first-pitch strike percentage. Our goal is 60%. Above 60% is excellent and a pitcher is doing their job—throwing strikes. Too many pitchers think their job is to get outs. We always tell them if they throw 60% for both first pitch and 60% overall strikes, then we cannot be disappointed in their outing, and they should not be either. As a season proceeds, these stats are useful in helping make a decision about who might be your best guy to use in a big game in relief, or in comparing two players for which one might be your number one. When a reliever comes in, chances are there are runners on and it is a pressure situation. You want a guy coming in who has a high strike percentage. Keeping track during the season will help you make an informed decision intsead of going with your gut in this case.

5. QUALITY INNINGS

The definition of a Quality Inning is any inning in which a pitcher throws thirteen pitches or less, or has a one, two, three inning regardless of how many pitches it took to get three out. (Most of the time the one, two, three inning is recorded in less than 13 pitches, but not always.) Once I started using Quality At-Bats and found that the System was a great one to use, I knew I needed to create something for our pitchers that was process-based, as well. So the Quality Inning was born. If you are wondering why I settled on 13 pitches, it is just simple math: 7 x 13 = 91. That is, if our starter threw 7 out of 7 innings as Quality Innings, which has happened but is rare. This gives the pitcher 9 pitches to get to 100. I hate to put a number like 100 on a pitch count because I would rather look at the situation and the individual pitcher's strength, but as a general rule, I feel most coaches are going to start to monitor things a bit more closely once the 100th pitch is near, even if the pitcher has been cruising through the game to that point.

This seems like a pitcher-only PPI Statistic, but I look at it as a team defense stat. Yes, the pitcher gets credit for the Quality Inning, but the team must make plays to allow for thirteen pitch innings. If there are errors committed during the inning, it makes it that much more difficult to get a Quality Inning. So, we talk about the Quality Inning as a measurement of, not only the pitcher, but also the team's defense as a whole.

Benchmark

Our goal for each game is for our pitchers to have four of seven Quality Innings within the game; anything higher than that is outstanding. The core values we hold to be true are to work ahead, stay ahead, keep pitch count low. We are always measuring. Remember, measure what you treasure.

1. **Work Ahead** – Measured with First-Pitch Strike Percentage/A3P

2. **Stay Ahead** – Measured with Overall Strike Percentage

3. **Keep Low Pitch Count** – Measured with Quality Innings/ A3P

With these three tools, we are breaking the inning down into segments and are able to pinpoint any deficiencies in our game.

If looking to start somewhere with your pitching staff, I would say that the First-Pitch Strike Percentage, Overall Strike Percentage, and the Quality Inning should be mainstays in your program. I think you will enjoy the conversations they bring about. Focusing on the process also keeps your bench players involved in the game. (Remember they are going to be the ones doing the charts after you teach them how)

 Visit www.1pitchwarrior.com/free
for BONUS *1-Pitch Warrior* Tips
& FREE Systems of Success

For those of you looking for more, or already using something similar to Quality Innings and Strike Percentages, then the next tool to measure a pitchers' performance may be what you are looking for.

6. S.T.R.1.K.E.

S.T.R.1.K.E. is to a pitcher/defense what B.A.S.E.2. is to offense. Again, we covered the significant impact the B.A.S.E.2. System can have on the outcome of the game, if you get three of the five criteria. What we wanted to do was develop something that was similar to B.A.S.E.2., but for the other aspects of the game. Even though I love B.A.S.E.2., it is one sided—all offense and we know that it takes more that just a great offense to win games. What we (Coach Jon Fitzpatrick and I) came up with was a scoring system that is easy to remember for both coaches and players for our defense and pitchers. Here is what the S.T.R.1.K.E. System stands for:

S = Shutdown Inning (+2)

T = Thirteen Pitches or Less (+1)

R = Retire First Batter of Inning (+1)

1 = 1, 2, 3 Inning (+1)

K = Strikeouts (+1 for each)

E = End the Inning (+1)

This is an actual scoring system instead of just a check-off list like B.A.S.E.2. Definitely a little more work for a coach, but well worth the feedback it provides to your team. Just to note, this is something that you could do with all pitchers during the game, but what we have found is it is best for just the starter to determine if the pitcher had a Quality Start.

Let me explain why we decided on the six factors that make up S.T.R.1.K.E. and why we award the point values that we do. Before I get into each category individually, let me say that these were chosen, because we felt that by doing these things defensively, we would greatly increase our chances of winning. We wanted to keep the list short. I have read what some pitching coaches are trying to do and the list is endless, it goes on and on. I cannot remember more than a handful of things and I am certain most players are the same. If we can consistently have Shutdown Innings, Quality Innings, Retire the First Batter, have 1, 2, 3 Innings, Strike a few batters out, and End the Inning once we get two outs, our starter will be giving us a great chance to win the game.

Shutdown Inning

As you have learned with B.A.S.E.2., Answering Back is a part of the game that can increase your chances of winning. Offensively we are tying to counter. When the other team scores in any half inning we want to score immediately in the next half. The reason we decided to include the Shutdown Inning was we are trying to prevent that from happening to us defensively. If we score, then put up a zero after we have scored. Essentially, we are trying to negate the other team's ability to collect the "A" in B.A.S.E.2. Because the chance to shut the other team down does not happen every inning, we felt it was important enough to award it two points. For example, if we score the game's first runs in the bottom of the third inning, then our defense/pitcher has the chance to record a Shutdown Inning in the top half fourth inning. If we do put up a zero, then two points are earned in that inning, and any subsequent inning, when this occurs. The biggest difference between B.A.S.E.2. and S.T.R.1.K.E. is that B.A.S.E.2. is a one-and-done, whereas the criteria of S.T.R.1.K.E. can be earned multiple times throughout the game. It is a scoring system rather than a check system. Aside from the Shutdown Inning, pitchers have the chance to earn points in each category, every inning.

Thirteen Pitches or Less

As previously mentioned, we want to work short innings, keeping the pitch count low for the inning and down for the game. Every time a pitcher records thirteen pitches or less, they receive one point.

Retire First Batter of Inning

The data I have found for MLB state that, if the leadoff batter gets on, he scores over 37% of the time. I am sure this number increases as the level of baseball/softball moves from college to high school, or even younger. So, to try to avoid this issue, we make sure we give credit to our pitchers when they do retire the lead-off hitter of an inning. Again, it is one point for each time they record the out of the first batter.

1, 2, 3 Inning

Any time the pitcher records a 1, 2, 3 Inning, we give him a point. This is in addition to having a Thirteen-Pitch Inning, because a Thirteen-Pitch Inning might have more than three batters—could be four or five. Also, a pitcher might record a 1, 2, 3 Inning and throw more than thirteen pitches. What we do is split apart what I previously called a Quality Inning and award a point for both (Thirteen or Less/1, 2, 3) parts individually, since they are not mutually exclusive.

K—Strikeouts

I have made a big point about not telling our pitchers to try to rack up strikeouts. But we felt it must be approached as a part of S.T.R.1.K.E., due to the fact that baseball and softball are much easier when your defense does not have to make plays. Every K recorded is an easy out and also worth one point within the S.T.R.1.K.E. System.

End The Inning

We added this because the most frustrating thing for coaches is to see the pitcher cruise through the first two batters, then lose focus and walk the third hitter. We want to keep our focus and make sure players do not let up once two outs have been recorded. The strategy here is to create an inverse defensive philosophy to B.A.S.E.2. We are trying to score with two outs when hitting and we are trying to defend against it happening to us when pitching because of the significant impact it can have on the game. So, defensively our pitchers only get a point if they retire the very next batter once the second out is recorded. They do not get a point even if no one scores with two outs. An example of not earning a point would be the pitcher striking out a hitter for the second out and then giving up a hit and a walk, then the last out is recorded by a force-out at 2nd base and no one scores. We want to end the inning as soon as possible, meaning the very next hitter.

Benchmark

All things considered, the maximum a pitcher could score in any one inning would be nine points and that would only happen if we score in the previous half inning, giving the pitcher the opportunity to earn:

Two points for a Shutdown Inning	**+2**
One point for throwing thirteen or fewer pitches that inning	**+1**
One point for retiring the lead-off hitter	**+1**
One point for a 1, 2, 3 inning	**+1**
Three points for striking out the side	**+3**
One point for ending the inning	**+1**
Total Point for the inning	**= 9**

Obviously, a nine-point inning would be rare, but definitely possible. What we really look for is an average of 3.5 points per inning, or higher in the S.T.R.1.K.E System. Of course, we want to look at each inning individually, but we consider it a quality start by a pitcher if they have a 3.5 inning S.T.R.1.K.E. average, win or lose. We found 3.5 points to be the magic number when we rate starting pitchers with the S.T.R.1.K.E. System. We want pitchers to focus on process and this is a great way for players to have a road map of what successful pitchers do to give themselves a chance for good outcomes.

Here are the data that we have collected over the four seasons:

Quality Starts
(Having a 3.5 S.T.R.1.K.E. rating or higher)

The result was 82 wins, 3 losses, and 3 no decisions by our starters.

Non-Quality Starts
(Having less than 3.5 S.T.R.1.K.E. rating)

The result was 14 wins, 17 losses, and 9 no decisions by our starters.

This makes it very apparent that there are certain things that pitchers can do to improve their outings as a starter to have a quality start. The best part is now you can measure those specifics and provide constructive criticism to players in a loss and even in a win. As coaches, the worst thing we can do is give a pitcher a false sense of confidence when they really did not earn it. Coaching players openly and honestly with the mindset to provide ongoing opportunities to grow should be the goal for your pitching staff. S.T.R.1.K.E. can now be part of that.

7. FREEBIE WAR

Another great game-within-the-game that gives a glimpse of what the outcome will be in the end of the game is to win the Freebie War. Giving the other team an extra base within the game is never a good strategy. We want the other team to earn every single base. We try to minimize the number of walks we give up, the number of hit batters, the errors we make, and the ability to stop the other team from stealing bases. The strategy is completely the opposite for us—we want to draw walks, get on base from getting hit, capitalize on errors by the other team, and also steal bases.

We try to be on the plus side of each category:

For example, we draw 6 walks for the game and give up 3. We would be at a +3 for walks.

If we stole two bases, but the other team stole 5, then we would be -3 for steals. After looking at all four categories, we want to come out on the positive side of things. It is hard to win games when the other team has more Freebies than we do.

In a study conducted by Kevin Miller, which appears in the article he wrote for *Collegiate Baseball* in the April 2013 issue, found that over the years the team that gave up the fewest freebies won the game 89% of the time. He indicated that this statistic went up to 94% when they were winning the Freebie War by two or more. He also mentioned another statistic he found that falls right in line with B.A.S.E.2. and the Freebie War—big innings. A big inning is usually created by Freebies. Seldomly does a team create a big inning without a walk, error, wild pitch, etc. What Coach Miller found was that the team that scored the biggest inning or tied for the biggest inning won the game 95% of the time. This reinforces the idea that playing for the big inning offensively is critically important and minimizing the big inning with solid pitching and defensive play is so vital.

Other ways to further break down the Freebie War according to Kevin Miller are:

7 Pitching Freebies

1. Walk

2. Wild Pitch

3. Stolen Base

4. Error by the Pitcher

5. Balk

6. 0 – 2 Hit

7. Hit By Pitch

His list is a bit more extensive than what we use, but I really like the concept and depending on how complicated you want to get, you could use it for sure. He also created four ways for the team to deduct points from their Freebie total. Those are:

Four Deduction Areas

• Double Play

• Runners Picked Off (Pitcher or Catcher)

• Runners Caught Stealing

• Completing an Inning with Fewer than 10 Pitches

The Freebie War is definitely a strategy of success that can be easily incorporated into any program, at any level. Showing your players the result is also a very important part for any measurement to work. If you just record and do not share, that defeats the purpose, so make it part of your post-game conference, bus ride home, or pre-game meeting the next day.

8. T.P.I. – TEAM PROCESS INDEX

Team Process Index is a calculation that is based on a team's performance using key indicators that, in and of themselves, are very telling of a team's chance to win. TPI is a new and innovative way to measure the things that matter most and actually calculate how your team plays, without taking into consideration wins/losses. It uses many of the key concepts already mentioned in this book. It indicates how efficient a team has been during the game and will show strengths and weaknesses, not only in a single game, but also patterns throughout the season. It is based on process goals and all facets of the game (pitching, offense, fielding, and base running). TPI operates under the premise that if players consistently do certain things well, they will maximize their team's TPI Score and also increase its chance to win the game in the long run.

It is much like the first time you beat a video game. You understand the game, you know what it takes to be successful, and now the real game begins—not only to beat the game, but also to earn the high score for the game. I like to think of it backwards for baseball. We want to earn the high score for TPI and if we can, the chances are that we will win the game, or at least be satisfied with our performance.

We all know that one of four things will happen once the first pitch is thrown:

1. You will play well and win.

2. You will play well and lose.

3. You will play poorly and win.

4. You will play poorly and lose.

Having a tool, such as TPI, to truly evaluate play regardless of wins and losses is a better way of creating an environment of improvement. It lets a team move past the simple happiness of a win to focus on finding things that need to be improved for the next game so that your team has an even better chance of victory. If you focus only on results, you can get lost in the thrill of victory and be satisfied with what may have been a sub-par performance. Using the Team Process Index prevents this. It creates a dynamic of constructive criticism that will encourage growth within any program at any level.

What Makes Up the TPI?

There are 10 Key Indicators:

1. Error Differential

2. Walks/HBP Differential

3. Strikeout Differential

4. Stolen Base Differential

The B.A.S.E.2. System makes up indicators 5 thru 9:

5. Big Inning

6. Answer Back

7. Score First

8. Extend the Lead

9. Score with 2 Outs

10. The Quality At-Bat System

These criteria have been selected because they are measures of efficiency in all facets—pitching, defense, base running, and offense—of the game.

B.A.S.E.2. is a great indicator, in and of itself. Since the implementation of the B.A.S.E.2. System, our team has been 220-6 when we have recorded three of the five categories in B.A.S.E.2.

QAB is a great indicator, too. Since we began measuring our QAB % for each game, we have been 235-10-2 when we are above 60%, while only 50-25-4 when having a QAB % under 60%.

The bad parts about using only the QAB/B.A.S.E.2. Systems are that they are completely offensive. We (Jon Fitzpatrick and I) wanted to come up with something more comprehensive, multi-faceted, and also more reliable than just B.A.S.E.2. and QAB. Even though those systems are great, TPI is better.

How To Calculate TPI?

After looking at past seasons, on the data we have collected thus far, we found that a TPI above 48 points predicted a winning outcome 98.4% (126-2) of the time. The best part is that we did not factor our 88-game winning streak into the calculations. We wanted it to stand alone without those games inflating the overall numbers. On the other end of things, when teams were below 48 points, their winning percentage was just above .500. Again, we are not after the wins. I am most concerned with what do we need to do well to give ourselves the best chance for a win— the process. The point is, if you do these things correctly, then success may come your way. Winning is a byproduct of working this process. TPI can be a way to focus your entire program and communicate team philosophy. Especially at the end of games, going over the different parts of TPI helps re-emphasize the things your team did well that night and the areas of growth.

Each category is given a point value in the TPI system. You would receive positive points for the differentials of the four following areas: Errors, Walks/HBP, Strikeouts, and Stolen Bases.

As mentioned in the Freebie War section of the book, you would be plus 3 if you had one error and the other team had four. You would be minus 2 points if the other team earned six walks/HBP and we only had four. If we struck out 7 times and the other team struck out 7 times, then we would not earn any additional points toward our TPI Score. If we had a total of five stolen bases and did not allow the other team to swipe a bag, then we would earn 5 additional points in the Freebie category of TPI. These points will be either added or subtracted from your points earned within B.A.S.E.2. and the QAB Percentage.

If you fulfill a certain category within B.A.S.E.2., then your team scores 10 points for each. For example, top of first your team scores three runs. Your team would just earn 10 points for Scoring First and 10 points for having a Big Inning. Let's say that one run was scored with 2 outs, then you would get another 10 points. You cannot score more points if you have another Big Inning, or any of the others previously recorded. The most you could ever score off of B.A.S.E.2. is a total of 50 points. Remember that 48 is the benchmark to beat. So, if you had all of the possible points for B.A.S.E.2., then it would be your team's responsibility to keep your team's overall TPI Score above 48 by making sure it does the other things right, like hold runners, play good defense, etc. Because if they do not, they run the risk of letting their TPI drop below the 48 mark.

The last way to earn points toward the team's TPI is multiplying by 10 the team's QAB Percentage at the end of the game. Example: the team has a 55% Quality At-Bat Average; times that by ten, it would earn an extra 5.5 points toward the total. If calculating TPI sounds too confusing, we have created an easy-to-use worksheet for coaches to use.

Example of a Team's TPI Score

Freebie War:

Errors –	Us = 3, Them = 5, Result +2 for us
Walks/HBP given up –	Us = 5, Them = 9, Result +4 for us
Stolen Bases –	Us = 4, Them = 0, Result +4 for us
Strikeouts –	Us = 3, Them = 6, Result +3 for us
Total Point from Freebies =	+11 for us

B.A.S.E.2.

If the team has a Big Inning, Scores First, Extends the Lead, and Scores with Two Outs, it would earn another +40 points for its overall TPI Score.

Quality At-Bat Percentage

If the team goes 22 for 33 during the course of the game, this is a 66.7% clip. This is a great average. As it pertains to TPI, you would multiply the decimal .667 x 10, which equals 6.67. This is the final piece to the overall TPI Score.

Recap

+11 (From Freebies) +40 (From B.A.S.E.2.) + 6.67 (From QAB) = 57.7 TPI Points

This score alone would lead me to believe they won the game based on previous findings. Even if they did not, what a coachable moment it would be to know you played well, had a great TPI Score, and coach your team up.

The analysis is so easy that it can be done as you look over the scorebook in just a few minutes after each game. These data can be used to debrief your team after a game, which most coaches already do. You can now make this meeting more productive and go over facts, rather than rant about your feelings, and how play was "poor" or "great." Would it not make more sense to tell your team the specific things they either did, or did not do, that contributed to the game's outcome? I am not insulting any coach's intelligence by saying that individual players are not going to know overall what went well during the course of the game. TPI gives teams a much more systematic, fact-driven way of reacting to their performance. The numbers do not lie. Praise your team when its TPI is high, or they have set a season record. Give them positive, constructive criticism when things do not go well with TPI, as well.

When?

Start now! Why not use TPI? Remember: This not a way to gain more wins. It is a way to provide feedback to players and coaches. Such constructive criticism will help you continue to make strides in becoming the best. Let the data drive your decisions, rather than using subjective feelings that often get in the way. Stay focused on the process and not the end result with TPI.

To learn more about the Team Process Index and the complete *1-Pitch Warrior* System that provides even more innovative ways to create better systems and consistent play within your program, head to www.1pitchwarrior.com To schedule speaking or consulting engagements, contact Coach Justin Dehmer at coachd@1pitchwarrior.com

All of the Systems of Success (Ways to Measure the Process) are part of the *1-Pitch Warrior Guide to Mental Toughness* which, to help you implement these systems, provides access to all the charts along with the necessary spreadsheets to keep track of everything. Plus, with over 3 hours of video and over 2 hours of audio, there is no need to create it on your own.

 Visit www.store.1pitchwarrior.com
Order your copy of the *1-Pitch Warrior* DVD System to have all the resources at your finger tips to start creating *1PW*s in your program.

NOTES:

_____

_____

_____

_____

_____

_____

_____

_____

_____

_____

_____

_____

_____

_____

_____

_____

_____

_____

_____

_____

_____

_____

_____

NOTES:

PRACTICE DATA MEASUREMENT

"We want to hold them to the same standards in practice as we do in the game, maybe even higher."

– Coach Justin Dehmer

9. SITUATIONS – QABs

One of the best ways to teach your team about Quality At-Bats is to reinforce them at practice and measure them with the same criteria of nine Quality At-Bats they could earn during a game. The last part of our practice is always Situations. We create game-like scenarios such as runners at 1st and 2nd with a 1-1 count. The players have a chance to earn a QAB for that particular scenario—if they bunt the runners over, then QAB; or if they fail to move the runners, but hit a hard line drive to the centerfielder, then QAB; or if they grind out a long at-bat and foul a bunch of pitches off, put it in play, then QAB. You get the point. Players start to understand the system and truly understand what it means to have a QAB. They start looking out for each other and telling the coaching staff that was a QAB.

How it Works

We split our team up into 3 groups—one team hitting and the other two teams playing defense. If there are multiple players at a position, those players just rotate every batter, to stay focused. You do not want players waiting to make a play until they rotate. Keep them moving in and out.

The Situations might be set up in this way.

1. Runner at 1st	1-1 Count, 1 out
2. Runners at 1st and 2nd	1-1 Count, 1 out
3. Runner at 3rd Infield Back	1-2 Count, 1 out
4. Runner at 3rd Infield In	3-1 Count, 1 out
5. Runner at 3rd – Game Winner	1-1 Count, 2 outs

The rotation works this way: I have the teams posted with the order up for the player to know who is hitting and when. The first team to hit has the first 3 players listed be our hitters. The rest of the groups will have helmets on and be our runners to start at 1st base. The runners, the fielders, and the hitter play everything live. Typically, I am the pitcher or an assistant coach. We cut the distance down from the mound to home and throw behind an L-Screen. I mix it up just like a normal pitcher might— throwing fastballs, curveballs, and change-ups. I try to emulate the pitcher we know we might face next.

Once the first batter puts the ball in play he runs it out to 1st and the runner at 1st reacts to the hit ball, accordingly. Once the play is over, the hitter that just had his at-bat becomes the last runner at 1st and the runner who was live now becomes the last hitter in the rotation. This continues until all hitters have had an at-bat for that situation, then we move on to the next situation. If that happens to be runners at 2nd, then all the runners at 1st would move over to 2nd base. We are just trying to create as many different game-like situations for our team, as possible.

You can be as creative as you want with the situations and counts as you feel necessary. Things I have done in the past are all two-strike counts, all full counts, but to speed things up I typically always start with at least one strike on the batter. The number of quality-plate appearances for players is outstanding and the game-reps for the fielders are excellent, as well. I try to get at least four to five at-bats for every player on the team. If you have 21 players and each player gets five at-bats, then you have 105 at-bats that are good solid game-like situations. I have always been a firm believer that if we are going to hit on the field, it has to be in a live situation. We work out our mechanics in the cage.

One of the biggest advantages of doing situations is the opportunity to teach players about what Quality At-Bats are and to also start recording them for your team. My assistant or I (whoever is not the pitcher) keeps track of the QABs for each player and team on an iPad (on a spreadsheet I developed which is part of the *1PW: Mental Toughness Training* DVD). Because we have the data to back it up, we start to see which players are really performing well with the bat. We eliminate any tough gut decisions on which of two players who are competing for one spot should get it. I look at the overall numbers during our weeks of practice and let the numbers guide me on determining who earned the starting spot for the beginning of the season. I always feel like this is a fair way to make that determination. Our team and all players are evaluated on the same nine Quality At-Bat criteria and are even given the same number of at-bats during practices.

What this can do also is make practice that much more competitive. By recording each group's overall QAB on my iPad, we are able to give each team an up-to-date score of what their percentage is and how that compared to previous groups.

The three groups are always competing against each other for something. It could be conditioning at the end of practice, field clean-up duty, or anything else you decide on. The idea is to make it pressure-packed and see how they perform in those tough moments when they need a QAB to raise their percentage in order to beat the other team. We also hold the entire team to a certain standard each day at practice. Usually, early on, we might hold them to 60% for their QAB average, since that is the magic number when it comes to favorable outcomes. Once reached, I will bump it up to 65%, and so on, as the team is able to reach it. I want them striving and constantly pushing the limits to see how good they can be.

10. BUNT PERCENTAGE

The bunt percentage operates similarly to the QAB percentage. You set a target goal and see if your players can reach that particular goal. We always set our bunt percentage higher than our QAB percentage, as I feel it is much easier to get a bunt down and we want to make a point on the importance of getting bunts down when needed. Even when we were leading the state in homeruns and hits, we still worked the bunt game on a daily basis, because I knew as a coach, that one game sooner or later would come down to the ability to lay a bunt down and defend the bunt, too.

The one reason I love to record the bunt percentage is because then, all of a sudden, it matters to players. There are no freebies or just going to through the motions. I think, especially when it comes to bunts, a player's attention span is short and can quickly turn into something very counter-productive if you do not make it count. I tell them to split up into partners and work ten bunts each and then switch. I guarantee that five minutes into the drill there will be screwing around or a lack of true focus and effort. Make every bunt count on the field and instantly you create pressure on every bunt. I rather take three to five bunts on the field than have guys just going through the reps. A practice that is as game-like as possible has always been my philosophy.

Some ideas to incorporate into practice when it comes to keeping track of bunt percentage:

1. Set up cones to make sure the hitter understands the sections of field he needs to bunt to. I do not count it as a good bunt unless it is down one of the lines. Anything that is bunted hard back to the pitcher counts toward improving his overall bunt percentage.

2. Make your hitters go down both lines. Typically hitters seem to have a preference when it comes to getting it down. But, they need to be able to execute the bunt down both lines, depending on where the runners are on base.

3. Practice the squeeze, as well. When it comes to the squeeze, I am a little more lenient. I am more concerned with getting it down, than getting it down the lines, although it would be nice. I give the hitter credit as long as he gets it down and it stays fair.

4. Once we are in-season, I set our goal for bunt percentage as high as 90%. Adjust yours accordingly, but once a benchmark is achieved, always push your team to do better the next time. If the team does not make it, then they run three triangles—home to foul pole straight across to foul pole, then back to home under 1:30. If you really want to have fun, we do double or nothing for the triangles. If all the guys on the team get a sac bunt down with a 0-0 count, then they do not have to run, but if just one player does not get it done, then it turns into six triangles.

5. Not always, but typically, I give them two chances to get the bunt down if it was a sacrifice. The way I look at it is, if a player fouls the first one off in the game, there is a pretty good chance that I will still give him the bunt sign to get it down the next time. I want players to know how to refocus after not getting the job done, then step back in the box to attempt another sacrifice. On squeezes they only get one chance, no matter what.

There are various ways you can incorporate this into practice depending on how much time you want to spend on your bunts. Most importantly, you are recording meaningful data that can help you know who might be a good two-hitter, or a guy who could come off the bench to lay down a bunt for your team in a crucial situation.

1. The shortest way to do it is just a coach pitching (we liked to do it completely live from the rubber of the mound) and have each player get a bunt down first with all your players in the group. Then have them go down 3rd, and then a squeeze. You could repeat this as many times as you feel necessary. They would not run it out and there would be no fielders. Sometimes I use this as a station for our hitting rotation as another group is in the cages. To really save time, one thing you can do is have one hitter stay up to bat for all three bunts at once. I try to avoid this only because I really want to simulate a game at-bat instead of some drill where they are bunting fifteen balls in a row, which would never happen in a game.

2. Another variation to the bunting drill above is to have a group running the bases at 1st and 2nd base so they get a chance to read down angles off the bat and work on getting good jumps. One thing I like to do with this is to throw one high,

hoping the bunter takes it. I can see how the runners react to the pitch that is taken by the batter. If they keep going to the next base, I can tell pretty quickly which runners are just going through the motions. If I catch a runner going to the next base when they should not, then they run a triangle. I want the players to be alert on the bases and understand they are just as vital to this as the hitter is.

3. The longest variation of this is to add your infield, which allows you to work on the defensive side of things, as well. Making it completely game-like also allows you the chance to work on your defensive calls and the various bunt defenses your team may have. In terms of bunt percentage, if I have my corners crashing to try to get the lead runner and my hitter does his job and got the bunt down the line between the cones, then he still gets credit for a quality bunt, even though the infield made a nice play.

4. A nice thing to do is have your groups compete against each other in their overall bunt percentage for rewards or running.

Sometimes players seem to think that, when they are given the bunt signal, you have no confidence in them or they cannot hit, which could not be further from the truth. You are just playing the percentages and trying to get your runners into scoring position. What I tell our players about bunting is that it should be thought of as an honor and not a punishment. I use the analogy that we are parachuting to the ground and you are the one that gets to pull the ripcord saving the team from certain disaster. Use any of these variations at practice to create players who understand the importance of small ball and have experienced pressure to get one down in the big game for the upcoming season. Again, all the spreadsheets and charts are included in my *1PW* Mental Toughness Training DVD.

11. 50/100

After doing our normal ground ball work, I end with a drill I call 50/100 with the infielders. Depending on time, I count out 50 or 100 baseballs and then hit those balls, in random order, to the infielders who have to make the plays. Again, a game-like situation is what I am after and that is why I would randomize it. Most coaches will hit ground balls in order, from 3rd, then shortstop, then 2nd, and finish with 1st. I want all infielders to be ready to react when we do this drill.

We have one bucket of made plays and then one bucket of errors at first, so that once the play is over, our first basemen deposit the ball in the correct bucket. We get a quick fielding percentage this way and also can track our progress as an infield. We mix it up with the types of plays we are making. I might tell them to turn a double play and then hit a slow roller to my 3rd baseman. I mix in pop flies for communication between infielders. There is not any running or conditioning on the line with this drill unless you want to. I never do. I just want to stay away from monotony around the infield all the time. Once all the balls are hit, we count them up and see what our percentage is. If we have time, I use 100 baseballs, but, if time needs to be invested elsewhere at practice, we just do 50 balls. Kids like it and I always thought it was a good way to end our infield work. I also get an idea of where our fielding percentage is and we can start to measure progress throughout the year, too.

This can easily be done with outfielders too. Mix it up with fly balls, groundballs, hitting the cutoff man, etc. Be as creative as you want.

12. PRESSURE TIME

This is a great way to throw something unexpected at your

players. What you can do with this is create a scenario for your players to accomplish something that they will need to do in a game to be successful, such as getting a bunt down, or making a routine play to end the inning when the bases are loaded and the game is on the line. It is not scripted or in the practice plans so no one knows when it might happen, or who might have to come up big for the team. At any point during practice, you would call out "Pressure Time," select the guys you want to be involved, and set the stage for them to come through. Make them slow down the game; you are hoping to create tension and pressure. This is a great way for them to work on their mental approach and their routines.

For example, you might select a hitter to get a bunt down, a runner to get from 2nd to 3rd, an infield, and a pitcher to deliver a strike. The idea is everyone must successfully do their part, both on defense and offense, so that the team does not have to run or do some sort of conditioning. If they do not get the job done, the team pays up right then and there.

It can be as simple as putting your infield on the diamond and hitting a high fly ball that represents the last out to get to the state tournament that they must communicate on.

The idea is we win together and we lose together. Either way it is together. When the players come through, it is a great way to see excitement for their teammates and to build a sense of togetherness. Even when things do not go their way and adversity hits, it is still a chance to build each other back up.

During your practice time throughout the year, have every player on your team participate in at least one Pressure Time. Keep a checklist of your team and keep a record of who has had the chance to win a Pressure Time. If a player was not successful, come back to them later with that same scenario and offer them another chance to be the hero for the team.

13. BUNT DEFENSE

Being able to play small ball get the bunt down on offensive is a skill that all great teams need to have. I have seen more games lost because of a team's inability to execute its bunt defense to work an out. This is how many big innings start. A team throws the ball away for an error or it is out of position to even get an out.

Whatever your defensive calls may be for your team, the way you practice these calls and get outs must be at game speed and practiced often if you expect your players to know where to go and get outs when your team needs it most.

We do not necessarily record a percentage here, but you certainly could. We just do a certain number of successful plays in a row. We might say, "Today we must make five plays in a row before we move on to the next part of practice." The key here is we never settle for less than what we expect. It is said that you get what you expect. I remember a few coaches I had would just get frustrated with the way bunt defense was going and then they moved on to something else—never set a tone of excellence and never translated into good performance either.

What you want is to have your players rotate in and out, if you have multiple players and infield spots. Have your outfielders and runner/bunters. Sometimes I bunt the pitches and sometimes I let the outfielders do the bunting. If I am bunting, I actually let the runners start closer to 1st base to speed things up on the infielders. We rotate calls with the type of defense we are running, whether it is just looking for an out at 1st or crashing the corners to get the lead runner. We also incorporate our pick-offs here.

We work the drill as a run-through the first few times and then open it up to measure the performance. Once we get to the selected number in a row for that day, we are done. Pretty simple idea but some days it takes longer than others and sometimes frustration sets in, which is a good coachable moment for your players.

14. 1st AND 3rd DEFENSE

This tool is run in a similar fashion to our bunt defense. We look for a certain number of plays performed correctly. Once that number is reached that day, we bump it up to a higher number as the season goes.

What we do here is use the outfielders as runners at 1st and 3rd. We have the runners at 1st steal, not steal, walk off to create a run-down situation, and steal and stop halfway. Basically any scenario we have seen from other teams or have done ourselves. Everything is done live at full speed—quickly getting runners in position and rotating infielders to keep things moving. We just look for execution here, not necessarily outs. If our catcher makes a good throw to our shortstop and the shortstop cuts it off to throw back home because the runner at 3rd has made a break for it, and he makes a solid throw, but we do not get an out, I am okay with that, because we have done everything right. It just did not turn out the way we wanted.

15. TEAM COMPETITIONS

As you may have noticed many colleges across the nation are doing some sort of week they call the Omaha Challenge, or some other clever name that has obvious associations for where they want to be playing, come the end of the season. Most seem to spend a week at the end of the fall practice session to create competitive challenges that are not normal baseball activities. I absolutely love this idea and think it creates many positives that come from the not-so-traditional practice set-up. I can see at least 4 big benefits from this type of competition:

1. Get Players Competing

2. Get Players Away from Baseball/Off the Field

3. Creates Team Unity

4. It's Just Fun.

When it comes to athletics, we want players who are relentlessly competitive. When you really think about it, a great swing or a mechanically sound pitcher is worthless to your team if he has a 5-cent head and, when the pressure is at its peak, he breaks. Why not create opportunities for players to work on their competitiveness fostering growth and the chance to build that fire and desire to win outside the lines? Use the activities as a metaphor for how they will act during a game when it matters most and things begin to fall apart. How will they respond?

Any time you can get players away from baseball or the field, interesting things can happen. Leaders you did not know existed before can emerge. You also get to know your players on a more personal level, which is always a good thing. The events that you set up are ones that your team will undoubtedly compete in, but as smaller divisions within the larger group. There will be tasks that they must work to complete together. These tasks may be physically difficult, mentally exhausting, or some combination of both. In any case, the players are forced to work together and they will, because remember, they are competitors.

This atmosphere not only creates competition, it creates memories that players will remember for years to come. It is downright fun for all involved. Some of the players' favorite memories may come from the times the team spent outside the lines, or the times you spent away from traditional baseball practice.

The concept of the Omaha Challenge is a great one. For a high school coach it is tough to do, though. The team may only have two to three weeks to prepare for the season. In some states I have visited, even less. They cannot spend an entire week creating a challenge for their players, because every second is so very important in getting ready for opening day and the rest of the season. Also, getting players together away from the field might be tough to do. Perhaps you could manage once or twice, but much of this may have to happen at the field when everyone is together. To combat this dilemma, try picking only one task or competition per day that your team will compete in. I think the time invested for the 5-15 minutes per day will pay dividends for your team's camaraderie and level of competitiveness. The best time to do this might be right before your actual practice. To avoid injury, I suggest having your players stretch, warm up their legs, throw, and then get after the event of the day! This is a great way to set the tone of the practice to compete, compete, compete!

Set your team up in what you feel are equal teams and let them have at it. I would suggest creating a scoring system for each event. (More on this later with what we have created.) Have them compete every day and keep track of the score. Announce it at the beginning of every practice. Let the players know what they are playing for in advance. It could be something like a team dinner where the losing team(s) has to serve dinner to the winning team(s). Maybe the winning team does not have to carry the gear for the entire season. Be creative with it and make it fun. You could even make it a daily thing, like no field work that day for the team that wins. Or, less conditioning and then still do a total for the practice sessions with an overall winner at the end.

Here are some ideas for events you could use and incorporate into your own "Omaha Challenge:"

Tire Run – As part of a relay for their team, players hold the tire above their heads while running a certain distance. The winner is the team that finishes first, but other teams still compete for second, third, etc.

Tire Wrestle – Put a tire out in the middle of the infield or at 2nd base. Each player starts at 1st and 3rd and the first player to bring it back to his base is the winner. You could use this as a tiebreaker. Match up similar strengths.

Cinder Block Walk – All players on a team get a cinder block for each hand and they have to get it across a certain point. The fastest time wins. I make the distance long enough so that players really have to struggle with burning forearms and potentially have to stop to set down the blocks.

Tire Throw over the Outfield Wall – Have each team throw a tire up and over your outfield wall. Use a set number of throws. All teams could compete at once, or best time wins.

Log Run – Each team holds a log above its heads and must get it across the finish line.

Log Flip – Set a certain number of flips and each player must flip the log. Then take a team total.

Squat with Med Ball Pass – The players are partnered. Each player does a set number of squats with the pass to the partner. Squat pass, squat pass, etc. This is a timed event.

Gator Push and Pull – Put the team's Gator at home and in neutral. Have half of the team push it to 3rd and then the other half of the team pull it back to home. Do this as many times as you want. This is a timed event.

Abs – Create ab events in which the teams have to outlast each other like planks. Teams get points for the position they finish. Individuals get points for which place that their team members finish. Example: First Place = 10 points, Second Place = 9 points, on down to 0 points.

Bench Hops – Using the bench in your dugout, players hop up and down in a certain amount of time, or time them until they reach a set number of hops. Most hops or quickest time wins.

Relays – Create relays to do indoors that combine abs, sprints, and other moves to make inside workouts/conditioning more productive than usual.

Obstacle Course – Use a combination of any of the events mentioned above to create an obstacle course that players need to complete.

Blindfolded Puzzle – One player is blindfolded and another gives that player verbal directions—no touching—on which piece to pick up and where to put it. Seems easy, but it is not. Use baby puzzles and watch your players struggle. Communication is key.

Baseball Trivia – This is another great game that can be played when it is raining and you are forced indoors. Come up with questions about rules, baseball history, and your program's history. Test your players' knowledge.

Concentration Grids – If you have not checked out concentration grids from Brian Cain, this is a great way to practice focus. Time each player on how long it takes him to finish. Best times win more points for his team.

Other ideas that can be played away from the field are Tug of War, Bowling, Swimming, Football, Karaoke, or Dance Competitions. (use a Wii or some other video game console and let your team have at it).

I have talked with Coaches who have a practice and then a sleepover at the school. This would be a great time to incorporate many of these contests for starting off the season and to begin instilling in your players the mindset for competition while at the same time building a sense of team.

If you have ideas on what you could do, or are currently using in your program, I would love to hear about them to share with other coaches. You can either email me at coachd@1pitchwarrior.com or post them on my website 1pitchwarrior.com under Blog "Omaha Challenge." Then check back for other coach's ideas.

If you would like to see a spreadsheet you can use to keep track of each team's progress throughout your challenge, go to www.1pitchwarrior.com/teamchallenge to download it free for either your iPad or your Windows-based computer. All you have to do is title each event, put the score in for each player competing in the event, and the spreadsheet will award the first place points to the winner and a percentage for each player thereafter. It will also keep a running total for all events.

16. TRIANGLES

Any player who has ever played for me knows what a triangle is. The other thing he knows about a triangle is how much he completely hates it. I have always used extra conditioning as a way to motivate players. Let's face it, no one really likes to run. It is a necessary evil. Our practices are fast-paced and conditioning is built in, if we go full speed. But the triangles are always earned if the players are not completing certain parts of practice correctly, or at a certain percentage, as mentioned in the Quality At-Bats and Bunt Percentage portions of this book. I also use them for when players are late to batting practice or any regularly scheduled practice. The players are not allowed to participate in practice until the "debt" is paid. I remember once, I was about 5 minutes away from leaving three players behind on a bus trip to an away game, because they could not make it on time. They eventually did.

In a triangle, players run from home to the foul pole, then directly across the field to the other foul pole, and end at home plate. We also call them one in one-thirty. Simply put, it means that players must finish one triangle in one minute and thirty seconds. To make it a team-oriented task, every player must make it under time, or we do another one. I suggest you test out the time and adjust it accordingly. You may have a huge field or a really small one, therefore, adjust your time so that all your players are able to make it. Record your top triangle times to keep the players at the front motivated to push themselves. You do not need to use triangles, but this was my thing that worked well for me and my players.

17. TIME YOUR INFIELDERS

Once the ball is hit, have a coach, injured player, or team-manager use a stop-watch to determine the time it takes for the infielder to get the ball to 1st. I start with just over four seconds being the time to beat. If this time is no problem, then keep lowering the time to beat. Clock the fastest players you have from home to 1st and practice at this speed. This way if your infielders are confident that they are able to get the quickest player, the remainder will be no problem. It also helps players understand exactly how much time they really do have to make a play. They start to develop an internal clock about how much time they have exactly. How many times have you watched a player take a ball out of their glove and rush the throw only to make an error?

This is an easy way to add pressure to your infielders, whether they are going to 1st, or turning a double play. The person on the watch should call out the actual time every time so that players know how close they are to your desired time.

18. TWENTY-ONE

This is one of the easiest ways to measure your defense—get twenty-one outs in a row. It is a simple concept, but difficult to execute at times. We ask our players to make 21 routine plays in a row. With good pitching and solid defense, we always know we will be in the game. The message here is clear. Make the routine plays until we get twenty-one outs. If we are at nineteen and an error occurs, we go back to zero. Then, the next ball is hit right back to the player who committed the error. I found that a great way to work on the mental part of the game is having the player go through his routine to flush it and use the "so what, next pitch!" mentality, because I am going to hit it right back at him. He knows this. I need concentration in the present moment, not on the previous play that was just booted.

Again, this tool is a way to accomplish something significant and we do not move on until twenty-one outs are recorded. If it takes an hour, then it takes an hour, and we just cut out hitting at the end of practice. Hitting is always last and held out in front of the players like a carrot, because let's face it, all players love to hit—that is usually their favorite part of baseball or softball. But, my favorite part of coaching is being completely prepared for all facets of the game. Defense comes at a premium ever since the inception of the new regulations of BBCOR bats. The College World Series is a perfect example of how the game has changed. Great pitching, coupled with defense and a few timely hits have been the difference-maker the last few years. Defense is at an all-time premium. The slugfests of the past are over. I feel this same concept will certainly trickle down to the lower levels, too.

Anything you can do to challenge your team to play excellent defense will make you that much better. Getting good reps in during your infield/outfield work is great and serves its purpose. But twenty-one puts the spotlight on that player to come through when the team needs it to get one out closer to twenty-one. Pressure is certainly there and, when they do not make the play, the feeling of failure will be there, too, which in turn, allows players to respond to adversity instead of react to it.

Players need to know that it is possible to play an entire game of flawless defense. Pitchers will also gain confidence knowing there is a good defense behind them. When pitchers are trying to do it all themselves, it usually results in a poor outing. Pitchers need to have confidence in pitching to contact. Let the other team hit the ball and the defense will make the necessary plays. Sandy Koufax once said, "I became a good pitcher when I stopped trying to make them miss the ball and started trying to make them hit it." Bottom line—pitch to contact!

19. C/R/Ts (CUT-RELAY-TAGS)

Another important part of the defensive aspect of the game is being able to get runners out on relays or, at minimum, be able to hold them to the bases that they have earned without giving any extra 90 feet due to a dropped relay, poor throw, or ball that is not picked/blocked at the bag. We look for the entire process to be clean, from beginning to end. Typically, we do this with no runners, but as we hit the post-season we may use JV players as runners to make it completely live.

We put all the outfielders at their positions and have the infielders at their spots, as well. I usually either hit or throw balls from behind the mound and create situations for the outfielders. For example, I may hit a ball against the fence down the left field line and have the relay to 3rd, then immediately hit a ball in the gap in right-center so that the centerfielder and right-fielder have to communicate with each other, and then relay the ball to 2nd base. I try to have two relays going on at once. It is just more effective and we get more work in quickly. I continue to switch up the situations with the outfielders until we have everyone throw to 2nd and 3rd.

Once our pre-work is done, the measurement begins. We will give our defense a certain number of errors and continue to have the outfielders work with our infielders to make go relays and tags. If a middle infielder catches the ball, makes a throw and short hops the 3rd baseman, and they do not pick it cleanly with a tag, that would count as an error. They would be down one error. If they only had three to cash in that day, they would be down to two left. If they made no more errors along the way, they would be at zero, and every error after zero would be a triangle they would have to run. As we get closer to the season, or are in-season, we back the number of errors down to two or one. I very rarely start them at zero. But, I hold them to high levels of excellence. We go through the entire process until all outfielders have thrown to 2nd and 3rd.

Typically we do not have them throw to home, as our catchers are usually doing their drill work at this time, but from time to time, we have them throw to a cut-off man with a relay to home at the very end of this part of practice. This saves their arms a bit and is not something I feel we need to do everyday.

20. BATTED BALL EXIT SPEED

A great way to give hitters something to strive for is not just bat speed, but how quickly the ball jumps off their bat especially if you work with your players on an off-season program that may include weight lifting and over/under loading for strength, too. Measure every player five times on just some simple sort-toss with pitches he can drive back through the middle. Keep someone standing behind the L-screen to measure the speed and record each hit. Take the average of the five-batted balls and now you have his baseline for other measurements down the line. Re-test them throughout the off-season and, again right before the season, to measure the progress. I think it is a great way for players to start seeing the rewards of an off-season program you may be utilizing. We measure our pitchers' velocity all the time and want them to continually throw long-toss and hit the weight room to develop a strong lower half and core. They certainly get excited when they make a jump by a few MPH from one year to the next. Why not try something like that with your hitters?

21. BLUE DEVILS 10

One of the things I always had a hard time understanding when

I was playing baseball in high school and college was what really was going on when the pitching coach was working with pitchers in the bullpen. I know they were probably working on mechanics and making adjustments but what really dictates whether it was a good bullpen session or not? Does coach just tell everyone, "Great job!" when they are done?

My math background helped me come up with a better way to evaluate your pitchers' bullpens in a competitive environment called Blue Devils 10. In this game we play with our pitchers, and have them chart all balls and strikes. I feel it is vital to show pitchers what is really going on so adjustments can be made if they are not hitting the benchmarks we talked about earlier. (Remember, 60% strikes is what we are shooting for.) If they are throwing 60% strikes with an unorthodox delivery, but still getting the job done, I may hesitate to make mechanical changes to that player because he has obviously figured out how to get it over at a rate that makes me comfortable. If he is not hitting the 60% mark, I now have some ammo to show him when I discuss making some changes mechanically, mentally, or both. As we keep working our Blue Devil 10 Bullpens, we get to continually test them and have measureable feedback on whether our players are improving.

Here is how the game works:

1. Split up your pitchers up into groups of three to five. Each group will be throwing together on a mound. You can adjust this according to how many pitchers you have and how many mounds you have available. We usually do this indoors during the winter and have three to four portable mounds going at the same time. But it is not uncommon to do this during the season and post-season, too.

2. Each player gets a sheet and something to write with before their bullpens start so they can chart their balls and strikes.

3. Basically, it is like pig for pitchers. They are finished with what we call an inning when they have thrown ten strikes. The first pitcher to throw ten strikes wins. The important thing to note is that all pitchers need to continue to play it out for all other places. Once guys get to ten strikes, they wait until everyone else is done. If it takes twenty-four pitches, then it takes twenty-four pitches. This game will expose pitchers for what they truly are.

4. The rotation works this way with what each pitcher will throw. First pitcher throws fastball; if he throws a strike then the next pitcher would throw a change-up. If he hits for a strike, then next pitcher throws a curve. If he threw a ball, the next pitcher throws that same pitch (in this case curve). Basically, we throw that pitch until someone throws a strike. In the beginning of the pre-season, we may only throw fastball and change, eventually mixing in all pitches.

5. After the groups are all done, we mix up the groups. First place guys will compete against each other, second, and so on. Have them go another "inning." We want them competing against each other, and also against their personal best. If a player throws ten strikes in sixteen pitches, they will be above the 60% strike benchmark that we strive for. Obviously we would like to see lower numbers, considering there is no umpire and typically no one standing in—although once official practices start we like to do that. We continue up the number of rounds we do each week.

After the night is over, I collect the sheets from all the players with their names on them. I record the information in a spreadsheet that I have on my iPad. It helps me keep track of each individual's progress, to see what his best pitch is, and it also gives me the ability to email it or print it out for the player. I arm myself with knowledge about each player. I know who might be a better guy to come out of a relief role, who can throw strikes immediately. Best of all it aligns with what we preach to our pitchers…throw strikes.

At times I might call the balls and strikes for a particular mound. I like to squeeze the zone and see how they react or respond. If they are they going to question me at practice, chances are they will react in a similar fashion in the game, too. If I am not calling balls and strikes, then the catchers do.

If you are interested in the data collecting charts or the data recording spreadsheets for Blue Devils 10, you will find them in the *1-Pitch Warrior* System, along with all the other charts I discussed earlier. Go to www.1pitchwarrior.com to purchase the *1-Pitch Warrior: Mental Toughness Training System* DVD and my 1st book *1-Pitch Warrior: Mental Toughness Training System.*

22. BELOW THE STRING

Another game you can play in a similar way as Blue Devils 10 is put a string that cuts the strike zone into the two lower thirds and the upper third. What we look for here is for players to stay low in the zone where they are less likely to get hurt with extra base hits.

There are many variations of this that you can run.

1. You can do the first to ten below the string like Blue Devils 10.

2. A certain number of pitches and record how many are below the line.

3. Work it with all pitches or just fastball.

4. If you want to get really into location, you can have players work on a high fastball for an out pitch when ahead in the count.

5. I have talked with some coaches about even breaking the strike zone into 4 sections with a horizontal string and a vertical string. They play the location game. Much like pig. I throw it here; you have to match me.

The point again is we are having players compete against each other by reinforcing what we want—getting the ball over the plate.

23. 5/5/5

Aside from the previous bullpen sessions I have mentioned, the only other type of bullpen I have run is a 5/5/5. It is basically a scripted bullpen. Pitchers throw fifteen pitches and then do something, like a set of lunges and abs, get back in and throw another set of 5/5/5. The five pitches can be whatever you want. Early in our winter work, we might just throw five fastballs followed by five change-ups and finish with five more fastballs. The important part to understand is that even these are charted for balls and strikes. The reason I settled on fifteen is because it is slightly above a quality inning. I do not want pitchers simulating the worst inning of their life by throwing a bullpen of thirty or forty pitches.

Some other things to note are that pitchers are matched up with other pitchers. So, one pitcher throws a fastball to another pitcher, the receiving pitcher then pitches a fastball back to his partner. It is more efficient this way. After the set of five pitches are over, the pitchers mark set round of five pitches on the sheet I give them prior to their pen. Typically we do this on flat ground.

What we have found as a good way to work is to do a few 5/5/5 rounds and finish the pitching sessions with a Blue Devils 10. I like to mix up with what we do, but always finish with something that is competitive and record balls and strikes to provide that feedback for our coaches and especially our players.

24. MORE TEAM COMPETITIONS

I have already talked about splitting your team up into smaller teams for fun competitive activities, but what we do at practice is keep the groups the same, so not only are they getting points for the activities, the teams also compete for points at practice during other baseball related events like Situations, Bunt Percentage, Pressure Time and Smash and Dash. I like to use three different teams.

It keeps things easy at practice, because I never have to make groups—they are already created before the season ever starts. I try to make the teams as closely matched, as possible. For example, each team works its way through Situations and we record the results. The team with the highest percentage wins another point for the team, for that particular part of practice. We let everyone know who won. It works the same for Bunt percentage. Pressure Time is a way for that team to earn another bonus point for the team that day. If they get the job done, they earn a point; otherwise no point. Smash and Dash is when Team 1 is hitting and two other teams are in the coach's boxes ready to run after the batted ball. There are no fielders and the hitter only gets one swing, so they have to hunt a good pitch. After the ball is hit, the hitter runs the bases and one player from the 1st and 3rd coach's boxes runs after the ball. Once both of them touch it, points are awarded to the hitting team for the number of bases the hitter touched. If both defensive players touch the ball and the hitter is between 2nd and 3rd, then the hitting team gets two points. Players love this drill and it is a good conditioning drill since everyone is running his hardest. We usually rotate through no more than twice. It is just a fun tool that we used once in a while.

25. IDEAS TO MEASURE BATTING PRACTICE

Here are a few ideas on how to measure your batting practice to make it more competitive and tangible. The first is to simply take a hard hit average. Whoever is throwing batting practice can record each round. If you are giving each player five swings each round, it is easy to write down and also share with the players at the end of BP, or on the bus. You could even go so far to say that the tenth man off the bench earns the opportunity to come off the bench as a pinch hitter because he was not in the line-up, but had the hardest hit percentage. Even if you do not do this, it gives you a good idea of who hit well that day and may help you make decisions, once the game has started.

Another way to measure batting practice that is a bit more labor intensive but will give you a better idea of where balls are being hit is to rate every single hit ball on a scale from one to ten.

The scale would work like this:

Swing and miss or foul balls would not receive a point value. We only want to calculate based on balls put in play in order to get a feel for where players are hitting the ball and what types of misses they are having.

1 = Weak groundball that does not leave infield grass

2 = Groundball that gets to the infield

3 = Groundball that gets through the infield

4 = One hop through the infield

5 = Line drive to outfielder

6 = Line drive to outfield fence

7 = Home run

8 = Deep fly ball close to warning track

9 = Fly ball to outfield

10 = Pop up in the infield

Another thing we do to sharpen focus and try to be game-like during batting practice is the hitter only stays in if they hit a ground ball or a line-drive. Pop-up, swing and miss, and foul balls mean that they are done. The idea is to get to the sixth pitch. We call it the Sixth-Pitch Club. During games, the best pitch a hitter may see is the first pitch. Hitters must have their timing down right and their focus locked in. It frustrates me no end when hitters foul the first three pitches off and then square up to the last couple. The difference is in the preparation to the round of batting practice. It is based on a reward system, which I love. Players will start to get frustrated, too, if they keep getting out on the first or second pitches, which I love, too. This is a coachable moment where you can work on a process to flush the previous round and clear their heads to perform better on the next one. Players are able to work on managing the six inches between their ears while also trying to get to the sixth pitch.

Players who get to the sixth pitch can be rewarded with a piece of candy—something small, but significant enough to let them know it matters to you. You could also keep a running total for the season and see who gets to the sixth pitch most often. Reward them for their practice efforts at the end of the season at your team banquet or get-together.

The Power of Being a *1PW*

• Improves the quality feedback given to athletes to focus on player development

• Promotes discussions that are grounded in evidence and analysis rather than opinion

• Fosters collective responsibility for player success

Develop a shared mission or teams goals

• A commitment to continuous improvement

• Team developed goals

• Results in a collective responsibility

Collect Inquiry

• Consider the current reality regarding player's existing level

• Where are we now; where do we want to go?

• Examine and question the status quo; seek and test new methods and reflect upon the results

Continuous Improvement

• Persistent disquiet with the status quo

• Constant search for a better way

• Unwilling to tolerate inaction — always improving

• We turn aspirations into actions and visions into reality

Results-Oriented

- Focus on results to provide timely, efficient, and relevant information regarding player development

- People without accurate information cannot act responsibly

- People with accurate information feel compelled to act responsibly

To checkout the *1-Pitch Warrior: Mental Toughness Training System DVD* to help you implement everything you have read thus far and much more, head to www.store.1pitchwarrior.com to pick up a copy.

 Visit www.store.1pitchwarrior.com
Order your copy of the *1-Pitch Warrior* DVD System to have all the resources at your finger tips to start creating *1PW*s in your program.

NOTES:

NOTES:

NOTES:

Justin Dehmer

PRACTICE ORGANIZATION IDEAS

The following topics are all related to how practice is conducted and the ways to make sure you, your coaches, and your players are all on the same page ensuring you all get the most out of the time invested at practice. Some are simple ideas and others are actual parts of practice that could possibly be improved and done differently. You never want to fall into the excuse that this is the way we have always done it. I have heard many coaches say that over the years. Try new things— you potentially will get new results. I am sure you will be able to take a few of these tools and incorporate them into your next practice.

26. PRACTICE PLANS

When coaches see my practice plans they often ask why times are not listed. My response is I am not limited to or going to confine myself by time. One of the biggest mistakes coaches make is set a time for that drill, or that part of practice and, whether done well or poorly, they continue to move on to the next part of practice. I look at practice more as objectives we need to accomplish and, until they are done correctly, we do not move forward.

Another thing I do is post the practice plan before practice and expect players to know what the flow will be like so that we can transition from one thing to the next quickly. They need to know what groups they will be in, what drills we are doing, etc. I want practice to move fast. I actually want it to move faster than the game will. Taking a page from Oregon Football, practice faster than what you expect in the game. I hated baseball practices in high school, because it seemed like there was way too much standing around and never enough actual work getting done or improvements being made. Once I knew I wanted to be a coach, I started stealing great ideas from other coaches I read about, watched, or coached against.

I always make sure I have a copy of the practice plan printed for all of the coaches and myself. The one thing that all teams have in common is time. It is how you use that time which means the most. It is not the amount of time you put in, it is what you put into the time.

27. NAME EVERYTHING

One thing I realized early on was that every drill and each part of practice needs a name. Come up with creative names of your own, but having a name is vital when it comes time to transition. Having to explain the drill or the series of drills that you want your players to do every day takes up a significant amount of your practice time over the long haul. One minute here and one minute there really adds up quite quickly.

The part of practice that I think this tool can help with the most is your hitting stations. Without names for the drill, it turns into something else by the end of the rotation. It is like the game "Telephone" that elementary kids play. The message never stays the same and is always messed up by the end of the hitting stations. To take this a step further, put the names of your drills on pieces of paper and laminate them before the season. Then you can hang up the signs you want to do that day during practice or batting practice. The drill is far less likely to get messed up when the name is right in front of your players. It becomes easy to change your drills each day and to vary the ones you are using so you do not fall into a pattern of doing the same drills all the time.

28. DEFENSIVE SKILLS CHECKLIST

Before each season, I map out the skills that we need to work on for each player and his position. I break down each position into all the small details that make a good catcher or a good center fielder. I then set a goal for each particular skill. For example, we might want to block balls down the middle for a catcher 15 out of 15 practice days. Obviously, skills that are going to pay off more will get more reps and times devoted to them, but we do not want to overlook things, either. The coaching staff and I organize practices that allow us to get as close to the goals we set for specific positions. Rain and weather sometimes affect what we are trying to accomplish, but if we can work on skills indoors, then we will. I check off each skill after practice is over, or the next morning, but I like to do it as soon as possible so things are still fresh in my mind.

A few examples for a catcher might be:

Pickoffs to 1st, Throws to home on pass balls, Proper lane when throwing to 1st on a bunt or dropped third strike.

I highlight how many times we get to each on the spreadsheet and then check them off as we go. I like this for a few reasons.

1. It keeps the coaches focused on the skills we need to work on.

2. It is a great way to show players how much we have done and how prepared they are.

I have a tab for each position on a spreadsheet I created and one extra tab for Team Defense that does not necessarily fall into position category.

29. OFFENSIVE SKILLS CHECKLIST

The offensive skills checklist works just like the defensive checklist does. There are only two tabs in this spreadsheet, but the lists of skills are quite long. There is a hitting checklist and also a base running tab—an area that is often overlooked.

We decide what we want to do and how many times our upcoming team needs to perform those skills. You cannot just say that we will do what we did last year, because your team is not the same. You want to use this checklist differently every year. One year you may have no speed, so working on stealing bases may be pointless; whereas dialing it in on hit and runs may be a more practical use of time. Let your team drive what type of preparation you will need to do.

Both checklists are part of the *1PW* Mental Toughness Training DVD.

30. TWO DAYS DRILLS/FUNDAMENTALS, ONE DAY COMPETE

The way I set up practice is on a two to one ratio. On Monday and Tuesday, we work on all the little things—drill work in the cages, getting groundballs, fly balls, working on specialty defense, etc. I realize the importance of these and players, even at the high school level, still need much work on the fundamentals. What I want to do is create some sort of balance so that, after three or four days of the same thing, it feels like we are just going through the motions. If we work mainly on fundamentals on Monday and Tuesday, then Wednesday is a day that we just get after it and play games. Compete! Compete! Compete!

As I mentioned earlier, our teams are already set up so they are able to earn extra points for their team during the games we play. We might run Bunt Percentage, Situations, Hustle Game, and Smash & Dash. This way there are quite a few points up for grabs on the days we are going to compete. More points can be earned on the competing days than the fundamental days.

The Hustle Game is a scripted scrimmage with a coach throwing from a short distance. Unlike Situations where everyone hits, the Hustle Game is worked with three outs like a regular game. We might start the inning with runners at 1st and 2nd. The second inning might be runners at 3rd and 2nd. Typically we always start with runners on so runs can be scored and we can create defensive opportunities. We call it the Hustle Game, because after the third out is recorded, the next hitting team has 60 seconds to get everyone ready before the first pitch is thrown. If they are not ready, then I start throwing pitches and record strikes and eventually outs, if needed.

We play our strategies like we do in the game. If the runners are at 1st and 2nd, the first hitter that inning is going to bunt them over. I like to start with at least a 1-1 count on the hitter, but it is not uncommon to use a 1-2 count. I think it helps to make sure players are developing the ability to hit with two strikes. If we play three innings, the team with the most runs scored would win that part of practice.

During our Situations we actually are recording two different things that would be awarded points:

1. Each team's Quality At-Bat Percentage –
   Highest would win a point

2. Each team's Total Bases –
   Highest would win another point

At times, one team wins both, but not always. The reason we started keeping track of the total bases was it put more emphasis on playing good defense. If the defense is throwing the ball away and not making plays, then it is hurting its chances to win that point. Also, it also makes the offense run the bases that much harder, because it knows that if it hustles, it may not only get a quality at-bat, but also more total bases. Base runners also take more chances on the bases knowing that there will be no penalty during Situations for getting thrown out at a base. It can only help the team by trying to extend a single into a double, or a double into a triple. It also helps create defensive throws, back-ups, etc. which we want to be sure we can execute.

A typical week is:

Monday and Tuesday – Normal Fundamental Type of Practice with Situations at the end

Wednesday – Compete! Play games

Thursday and Friday – Normal Fundamental Type of Practice with Situations at the end

Saturday – Compete! Play games

Sunday – Off

31. HITTING IS ALWAYS LAST

Most players' favorite part of baseball is hitting. This is why we dangle it out in front of them like a carrot at practice. If they are unable to work their way through the other parts of practice that have been set up, we just will not hit that day. For example, if Twenty-One takes fifty minutes to complete, then we may not be getting to Situations that day. My personal philosophy is if we play good defense and have a pitcher who is throwing strikes, we have a good chance to win that day. We put a premium on defense at practice and expect it to be done excellently before we ever pick up a bat. If you think about the losses you had last season, I would venture to say that the majority of them were because of defensive miscues and poor pitching. Use the players' love of hitting to your advantage and to motivate the players to work through the parts of practice that may not be their favorites, but are necessary for success. Complete teams do not go through defensive and pitching slumps. Those two cannot take a night off. Sometimes the bats might go cold, but consistent defense and pitching are vital for any chance to hoist the trophy at the end of the season.

32. DO SITUATIONS DAILY

Offensively, I have yet to find anything out there that is as fast-paced as Situations, while at the same time getting good quality reps that leads to quantity, too. Think about this. If you have twenty players on your team and each one of them gets four plate appearances during Situations, you have eighty plate-appearances along with eighty opportunities to play defense in game-like scenarios. If you practice six times a week, and even if you only have two weeks worth of practice, you are going to get somewhere around 960 plate-appearances (80 x 12), which I feel is a conservative amount. I think it is reasonable to assume you could also get each player five plate appearances. Before we ever played our first game in 2012, we had 1,221 plate appearances. When it comes to quantity vs. quality, I always err on the side of quality, but Situations provide both and that is why I always made it a part of practice every day.

33. POST PROCESS RESULTS

One mistake coaches make when recording and charting things that deal with the game is keeping those results to themselves. This is like a teacher giving a test and never giving that test back with a grade to the students. The students learn nothing from taking the test and are left to wonder if that test was even important. If charting Quality At-Bats, A3P, Quality Innings, etc. are important to your team, you must show your team those results or they will never become part of the culture of your program.

Post results in the locker room or dugout bulletin board; email them to the team. Or my favorite method is to talk with each player on the bus and teach the process-based statistics to your players. Even if you post them, players are often left to try to comprehend what they mean on their own. If you tell them exactly what the numbers mean and what you are looking for, they become that much more valuable and your players will understand that they mean a great deal to you.

I try to talk players through the results at least once a week on a longer bus trip to or from an away game. This is especially important for freshman who have not been through it before with me. They are the ones who need to learn the system. Juniors and seniors will understand what they mean, so I just try to point out some positives about their hitting or pitching and coach them up a little. Try to give them that much more confidence about their progress at that point in the season.

I think you will find it very valuable for your players to post them, as well. Plus, it keeps you accountable as a coach to stay up-to-date with them if you tell your players that you are going to post results weekly.

Not only do you want to post for game results, but also your practice sessions, especially for the pre-season, as you begin to make those difficult decisions about who might play where or who is going to edge someone else out for the open-day start at a particular position. Let the numbers be your biggest guide. Your players can understand and respect that.

34. GATORADE GAME

The Gatorade game is used as a competitive challenge during an event of your choosing. The last man standing wins the Gatorade. This is how I work it with my infielders. I place the bottle of Gatorade on the mound. We hit groundballs and, if you make the play, you stay in. If you make an error, then you are done. I make it tougher each round while mixing in backhands, slow-rollers, etc. Players get competitive and it is a good way to reward them and yet, at the same time, it gets them to be focused on making plays, not just going through the motions.

Another way you could use the Gatorade Game is during bunts. Get it down, you stay in. Foul it off, or bunt it back to the pitcher, you are out. Each round you can throw a little harder or get closer to home plate, mix in curve balls, etc.

Any little way to get your players more focused and competitive is always a plus for your team. Find ways to use the Gatorade Game in your practices and the players will enjoy it.

35. POST-GAME CLEAN-UP RESPONSIBILITIES

Maybe this is me being way too organized, but when we have a home game, we always have players doing this, that, and the other thing. It seems they are never helping clean up the field. I have to boss guys around to do this job or clean up the dugout.

Finally what I did was make a list of all the jobs that needed to be done before we could leave the field. Then I assigned each player to a job. I told them that if everyone chips in and does his part, we would have it cleaned up in no time and they can see their families, girlfriends, or go home.

It works really well and if a job is not getting done, I know who to get on about it rather than shoot the entire herd. I have more job responsibilities, so I have some guys doubled up on jobs that are quick or easy to complete.

I also use this during our practices. Once we are all done, I give the players five minutes to clean up everything, get it all out away, and have the shed locked up and organized. If they do this under the time allotted, I take off conditioning at the end of practice. Once games or practice are over, the last thing I want to do is take fifteen or twenty minutes in a lazy slow manner to get everything squared away when, if we all helped out, it could get done in five. I want to go home to see my kids and the players do not need to be there any longer than they need to be.

36. HOW TO PREPARE FOR BATTING PRACTICE?

One thing I feel we are very good at is having a good scouting report on who we might be seeing on the opposing team each game night, especially if it is post-season. At practice and also during the day at batting practice, we try to replicate that type of pitcher. If it is a lefty who throws junk, then we get someone to come in who can throw that same way. Since none of the coaching staff is left-handed, that is the toughest one. We also make one of the stations in the cages a curve ball from a left-hander. We work on trying to stay on the ball and driving the ball to right field for our right-handed hitters. We want our hitters to feel very comfortable like they had already faced the opposing pitcher before their first at-bat begins.

After getting scouting reports or watching our opponents play, we gear our practices and day-of preparations to match the type of pitches they throw, the amount of looks they give runners, etc. We want to have a game plan at the dish and also on the bases. I am sure we won a state title in 2012 because of this tool. We knew exactly how many looks the opposing pitcher would do with runners at 1st and 2nd. We had worked on it and were able to steal two bases in the first inning, which led to the game's only run. You can never be too prepared.

37. PRACTICE STARTS ONCE WE GET IT RIGHT

This is huge. If you want excellence then you must demand excellence. Those that shoot for mediocrity usually get it. Champions understand that they must push themselves to be their absolute best, day in and day out, whether it is at practice, batting practice, in the weight room, or any other endeavor.

As a coach, if you are running a drill and the players are just going through the motions, not giving the effort you expect, or not making the plays needed, DO NOT move on to some other drill or the next part of practice. You are letting them off the hook—do not do it.

As I mentioned before in the Practice Data Measurement part of this book, you need to have a goal in mind for that particular day and hold them to it, no matter how frustrated you or they get because they are falling short. Adversity is a great teacher. How much more mentally tough will your team be if they find a way to get it done rather than moving forward without you pushing them?

Things like 21, bunt defense, 1st and 3rd defense are great tools to use to set goals which you can strive to achieve every day. Do not just go through the motions. Work with a goal in mind. Just fielding groundballs and taking swings in the cages does not prepare you for the pressure that players feel or put on themselves when the game actually begins. But, telling them they must achieve at a certain level does as close a job as I have been able to find.

38. HAVE PRACTICE PLANS DONE WELL BEFORE SEASON STARTS

Although it is a long and tiresome process to come up with practice plans that work well for your team, I always force myself to have them done at least a month prior to the beginning of the season. This way we still have time to tweak them as necessary. It also allows me time to ensure we include everything we feel is important in our practices with enough time to be ready for opening day.

I share these plans with my assistant coaches and we go through them together. During the span of our three straight titles, I had three different assistant coaches, so my role was always getting them up to speed and understanding the flow of practice. If they were not on the same page with me, it would show. I do not want to waste time and do not want the players to think we are just winging it. Practices usually last around three hours, but I feel like we get the most out of those three hours because of the pre-planning.

39. PRE-GAME THROWING ROUTINE

Rather than just going out and warming up, this is the exact practice plan I use for the pre-game throwing that is much more game-like for each player.

ALL PLAYERS

1. Rundowns – 3 Lines – 90 ft
   a. Ball out and up, no pump fakes
   b. Run as hard as you can
   c. Receiver is slowly creeping, flashes hand and glove when he wants the ball
   d. Follow your throw, but peel out of baseline

2. 5s

3. One-Knee Glove Pinch – 1 minute

4. One-Knee Catapult – 1 minute

INFIELDERS

1. 60 ft - Groundball position (ball in glove)
   a. 2 minutes
   b. Transfer, step in front, left, throw
   c. Receiver – double play turn as 2B

2. 75 ft – Groundballs same as above
   a. 2 minutes
   b. Follow throws

3. 90 ft – Backhands and Forehands
   a. 2 minutes
   b. Receiver – double play turns as a SS

4. 120 ft – Shuffle, shuffle, throw, follow
   a. 2 minutes
   b. Receiver – Relay man
   c. Hands up, catch it on glove side, transfer with arm fake

5. Max Distance on a line with one hop
   a. 2 minutes
   b. Crow Hop, Throw, Follow
   c. Receiver – Tags

6. Quick Catch – 10 in a row
   a. Team must be perfect

ALL PLAYERS

1. Rundowns – 3 Lines – 90 ft
   a. Ball out and up, no pump fakes
   b. Run as hard as you can
   c. Receiver is slowly creeping, flashes hand and glove when
      he wants the ball
   d. Follow your throw, but peel out of baseline

2. 5s

3. One-Knee Glove Pinch – 1 minute

4. One-Knee Catapult – 1 minute

OUTFIELDERS

1. 60 ft – Routine Groundball position (ball in glove)
   a. 2 minutes
   b. Transfer, step in front, left, throw
   c. Receiver – Relay Man with hands up

2. 75 ft – Non-Routine Groundballs
   a. 2 minutes
   b. Crow Hops, Throw, Follow

3. 90 ft – Fly Ball Perfects
   a. 2 minutes

      b. Work through the ball

      c. Receiver – Relay Man

4. 120 ft – Fly Ball Get Behinds

      a. 2 minutes

      b. Work around the ball, come through

      c. Receiver – Relay man

      d. Hands up, catch it on glove side, transfer with arm fake

5. Max Distance on a line with one hop

      a. 2 minutes

      b. Crow Hop, Throw, Follow

      c. Receiver – Tags

6. Quick Catch – 10 in a row

      a. Team must be perfect

For those of you who have, or are thinking of purchasing the *1-Pitch Warrior: Mental Toughness Training* DVD, there are five videos detailing the entire process of our pre-game throwing routine.

40. MORE THROWING IDEAS

These are some ideas on how to create a setting of execution and excellence during your throwing sessions at practice. We all know that if you start to measure something, players will start to take notice. It will start to matter. It becomes their motivation to do better than the day before. I always say that most games are won well before the game ever starts. If you watch both teams prepare, you can usually pick the winner in advance. These ideas to change the way we do things are not complicated ones, but rarely do I see them used. Use some of these ideas at practice, or even before games, to scare the hell out of your opponents and show them what type of team they are up against that day.

1. **NO CHASE** – It is standard practice that, once the ball gets by a player, he goes to get it and there is usually no consequence for an overthrow or a ball that is not caught. Since there is nothing riding on each throw, this part of practice can become very lackadaisical, mundane, and the game-like feel we want to create is not felt. To create some pressure, let us do a complete 180. Do not allow players when throwing to go get balls they miss. Instead if a ball gets by a player, for any reason, he leaves it and gets another ball from a coach who is ready and waiting to distribute balls when needed. To keep it simple, once the throwing session is over, coaches count the overthrown balls, record that number, and then impose some sort of conditioning like abs, sprints, push-ups, burpees, or anything else we can dream up. Imagine how much more concentration players will put into throws and how much better they will move to get into a good position to make a catch when they know every throw matters!

2. **OVER/UNDER** – Overthrown balls must be chased down by the player who threw it. The partner is also responsible for switching places with the player who launched it over his head. Unlike the overthrow, when a ball is underthrown, that ball has the chance to be caught. If we can get our players into good positions, they can pick-it or get a long hop. If the in-between hop eats them up, then both partners must do "something" you have decided on in advance. Make them pay up immediately—no rolling over push-ups until the end of the throwing session.

3. **QUICK CATCH** – Have players perform 5-10 throws to each other at 60-90 feet as a way to finish off the throwing

session. Time it for team records or personal bests. The last team must do an extra set of conditioning. Many times we do not stop until every group completes it successfully. If a throw gets away, we start again.

4. Another idea that is not really measurable but players like is to play music during the throwing sessions. It can liven things up and the session tends to be more upbeat if music is playing.

Again, the idea is simple. Make good throws or suffer the consequences. The recipe is good pitching + good defense = a chance to win. Emphasize this at practice, especially during your throwing sessions. Celebrate when they achieve team records.

41. HAVE A STEAL AVERAGE

Before every season, I have each player take an average size lead and then take off to steal 2nd base three times while we timed each run. It gives me an average on the speed of each player. I calculate the average for each player and put their times into a chart from fastest to slowest, laminate it, and have it in my back pocket.

This becomes a resource for me when I am deciding if a player can steal a base, or not. It is not a gut decision. I time the pitcher to catcher in between innings, then look at my laminated card to know where the cut-off would be. If I feel the catcher and pitcher are not giving full effort in between innings, I time the pitcher's time to home once we got our first runner on 1st base and estimate the catcher's best throw. I do the math and know which guys should be able to make it and which ones were on the bubble.

The combination of having players in the dugout charting looks the pitcher gives at each base and knowing which guys' average times would make it, was vital in my decision-making process. If you are coaching 3rd or 1st without a stopwatch in your back pocket, you better get one. It will make you a better coach.

If I am not getting a good read on the pitcher/catcher time to 2nd, then I send in a guy early in the game to steal, and get a reliable time that way. Obviously I send in a guy I feel can make it. A calculated risk is always better than a gut feeling. Numbers need to drive decisions for a coach. Arm yourself with a stopwatch and know what your players can and cannot do.

Visit www.1pitchwarrior.com/free
for the BONUS *1-Pitch Warrior*
9 "Innings" of Free *1PW* Training Resources!

NOTES:

NOTES:

NOTES:

Justin Dehmer

MENTAL GAME IDEAS

42. PRACTICE STARTERS

Look for ways to start your practice and give your players mental game lessons or life lessons—things that will emphasize what type of mentality you want your players to have on the field and once they leave your program.

I call them Mental Minutes or Skull Sessions. I always try to make these five minutes or less and have a theme to help them get the day started. I use audio clips, newspapers, magazines, and Internet articles—anything that I thought was a great story and would grab their attention.

Some topics of discussion are the following, but you are not limited to just these:

Have To vs. Want To, Routines, Adversity, Focusing on 1-Pitch-at-a-Time, Compared to What?, Loving the Grind, Working Hard and Smart, Reacting vs. Responding, Controlling What We Can Control, Perspective.

There is a wealth of information on this topic. Any time I find something in the off-season that I really like, I immediately put it in a folder to use once the season starts. I plan out the first 15-20 talks I will give at practices, and then as the season goes along, I review or try to underscore what we already talked about with a new story or perspective.

I always like to get the players focused on what we are trying to accomplish that day, that week, that season, and what type of people we need to be in order to make that vision a reality. Otherwise your players may just be go through the motions. The first five minutes you have their attention and you can pull them in and get them "into" practice. At the end of practice, they are tired and they do not want to listen; they want to go home after two or three hours of practice. Get them started correctly each day with your own Skull Sessions.

If you are looking for resources, try books by Brian Cain, Coach Bru, addicted2success.com articles, Success Hotline (Dr. Rob Gilbert leaves messages at this number daily 973-743-4690), or my first book *1-Pitch Warrior: Guide to Mental Toughness* includes many ideas.

43. PERSPECTIVE POSTER

We want our players to understand that the game of baseball/softball is exactly that, just a game. There are no life and death decisions made on the field or in the dugout. We want our players to develop the "Get To" mentality and stay grounded in the fact that playing is a gift to be cherished and not taken for granted.

One great way to do this is by creating a perspective poster with images from around the world that make you stop and think about, if going 0 for 4, or making an error that day, are really as big a deal as we make them out to be. You can make this a team event by asking each player to collect images off the Internet and bring them to your team session. To take it a step further, you can have each player create a more individualized poster with images of family and any struggles they have gone through. They could share their poster with the team. Although it may be tough for players to do, I think putting them in this possibly uncomfortable position is good for them to grow and a good way for the team to learn more about each other. Chances are you, as coach, will learn more about your players from this one session than you ever will on the field at practice.

I have each player keep these posters somewhere they will be seen every day. It could be at home, in their lockers, or any other place where it will be seen. The poster the team creates can be kept in the dugout and could even be taken with you on the road, too. Leave it in the bus, or take it in the visitor dugout with you. It just reinforces that the proper perspective is something vital for all players to take with them in all games they play, no matter how big or small the game may be. The bottom line is it is just a game and we want our *1-Pitch Warriors* to have the Compared-to-What? Mentality.

Personally, I do this activity every year. Sometimes I change the images and other times I do not. I add things that inspire me, make me think, or have made me a better person. Create your own. Here is my 2013 example:

PERSPECTIVE 2013

COMPARED TO WHAT?

44. CLEAR THE WATER

Let's face it, we all come to practice carrying that day's events—some good, some bad. Any number of things could have happened to your players that day—poor tests, failed a project, got in trouble in class, girlfriend issues, parent issues, money issues, the list goes on and on. The coaches are dealing with similar lists, as well. We all have to deal with many issues as parents, teachers, husbands/wives, and friends. We all wear many hats. The problem lies in the fact that often we continue to wear the wrong hat in the wrong situation. When your players are in class, no doubt about it, they should be wearing their thinking caps, but when it comes time to play or practice, they need to be focused on playing well and nothing else.

A way we emphasize this concept is a pre-practice activity called Clear The Water. I usually work the Mental Minute/Skull Session first. Then I break them down on getting focused on the task at hand, which is to put all effort and concentration into the next two to three hours of practice in becoming the best baseball team we can be.

This is the script for Clearing the Water

I start by asking the players to close their eyes. I talk while they are relaxed and I have them visualize filling up a glass of water. I say, "The glass is cloudy, foggy, and you cannot see through it. This represents all the problems of the day. As you look at the glass, things begin to settle and become more clear. Take your life and set it aside. Focus on the things you can control. For the next two to three hours, you are a baseball player. There is nothing you can do about school, family, or anything else. Let's clear the water, gentlemen. Let's get to work on being great and we can pick up the rest of our lives after practice."

I always feel this is a great way to focus the players because you really never know exactly what their day might have been like. I also enjoy it as a coach to remind myself to flush my own personal problems so they do not affect my coaching that day.

At the end of practice, we tell players to bang their spikes together. Knock the dirt off them. This symbolizes that practice is over. Good or bad, bad or good, they were done and now it is time to put our other hats back on. Go on being a dad, friend, brother, sister, student, etc.

45. ADVERTISE! ADVERTISE! ADVERTISE!

In the dugout, in the locker room, via texts, t-shirts, posters, etc., do what the best companies in the world do—advertise your message to your players continuously, even if it is only subliminally. I even blow up the perspective poster and put it up either in our dugout or field house. I put up mental game signs like "Flush It," "Win The Day," 'Trust Your Routine," "So What, Next Pitch," "Get B.I.G.," to name a few. Make the signs yourself, get them laminated, and they will last throughout the season. You can always update them for the next season.

46. HAVE A SLOGAN

Every campaign, whether it is a political one, a product launch, or a business, has a slogan. Every season needs one, too. I always want to go into the season having a slogan that sums up what we are going to be about. The coach in me enjoys coming up with creative ways to try to motivate the players and a good slogan is a great way. Some slogans were: Win the Last Game We Play, Refuse to Lose, All We See Is 3, and my personal favorite is—

If you read it left to right it says "Devil Baseball," when you flip it over

It says "Principal Park." This is where the state tournament is held in Iowa. The reason for this slogan was twofold:

1. We had to play our brand of baseball and stick to the process of playing Devil Baseball if we ever wanted to see the field at Principal Park.

2. I thought that it was also cool knowing that, when everyone else read the shirt, it would say Devil Baseball, but when the players looked down, it would remind them of why we were working so hard.

This technique is called an "ambigram" and you can have them made on a website called flipscript.com. This is a very interesting and great way to combine two ideas into one.

Another thing I do each year is create a video for the team in order to get the players to buy in. Let's face it, the type of players on today's teams are visual learners. You could talk to them all day about the things you want to accomplish, but showing them a four to five minute video and you can capture their attention for the entire season. No better example is the awesome video TCU makes every year to promote its program. My budget was never quite as large, but with iMovie I was able to capture what I was trying to get across. If you want to view the videos I made using iMovie, you can go to youtube.com and search "*1-Pitch Warrior.*" You should see all three videos and can use them to create your own ideas for your next campaign.

The last thing I do is create a poster for the team. I get copies made for each player to hang in his room or in his house. It includes the slogan and other sayings we talked about—our mental game vocabulary, if you will. I share the jpg file with them, also, so if they wanted to use it as a background on their computer or phone, they could. I always give them this before the first practice. Here is an example here of what one.

I sometimes go to players' houses for graduation parties or to visit, and it was always cool to see their posters up as a reminder of our ultimate goal. An added bonus was that the parents start getting into the *1-Pitch Warrior* Mentality, using the same language, too.

47. NOTE CARDS FOR GOAL

Something I have players do before every practice is to write down an offensive and defensive goal for the day. This was done along with a quick lesson reminding them that it has to be an attainable and process goal. I tell them that getting four hits today is not a good way to measure success, while hitting the ball hard in three of my four at-bats, would be both attainable and process-oriented.

I want them to have control of what they thought they needed to do to get better and it also gives the coaches an idea of what each player wants to work on, which at times, was dramatically different than what we have in mind. It becomes really fun to read them. I feel it keeps players more focused and gives them a good plan for practice.

If we know our 3rd basemen want to work on backhands, then we can help facilitate that throughout the course of practice. If I know one player wants to work on going the other way more consistently, then I can throw more pitches on the outer third to him and also during situations.

Again, anything you can do, as a coach that prevents your players from getting caught up in merely going through the motions or the mundane parts of practice, the better off everyone will be.

48. NOTE CARDS FOR AFFIRMATION STATEMENT

After the players have written down their offensive and defensive goals for the day, I have them write down one more statement. This is an aspirational statement—a reminder of what type of player they want to be and what kind of year that they want to have. I have heard many times, that people who write their goals down on a piece of paper and look at them daily, ultimately achieve those goals and desires. I did the same. I wrote down that I wanted to be a state championship coach long before I ever was one. Our players do the same thing. They write, "I will be a 2013 STATE CHAMPION." I believe when you write it down it gives you more conviction to go out and make it happen. It is a great way to advertise, advertise, and advertise.

I always have note cards and pens around before practice begins so players can fill them out, look at the practice plan, and know what is going on.

49. CREATE ROUTINES – WRITE THEM DOWN

Developing players who can focus on the moment and get totally locked in for big time games as *1-Pitch Warriors* is the heart of the routine. There are a couple of routines that every player should have scripted and know well enough so that when the game speeds up on him, it does not run away from him. The players are able to adapt to the adversity and event and will respond according to their plan/routine. The routine is a simple concept that helps players focus on what they are trying to accomplish and not let their emotions or thoughts get in the way and create a self-sabotaging situation.

The first type of routine is the pre-pitch routine. This consists of three things:

1. A Focal Point

2. A Deep Breath

3. Positive Self-Talk which is task-oriented, not outcome-oriented

All three must be employed for this physical process to unlock the mental. I will give you examples of routines for each part of the game and how your players can start to develop their own routines.

Hitting Routine:

1. Focal Point = Trademark on the bat

2. Deep Breath = Get B.I.G. (Breathe In Greatness)

3. Positive Self-Talk = Attack pitches in the zone or Drive a Strike, Drive it, Drive it

Players cannot rush their way through this process. They cannot fake it. Remember, in earlier lessons, we talked about only being able to focus on one thing at a time. The focal point is going to help us do just that. If I just had a bad call and if I am truly locked into the bat's trademark, I will have a hard time thinking I just got screwed on the last pitch. Call it distraction control for out hitters. Once total attention has been given to the focal point, the hitter gets that big deep breath to relax them. Relaxed muscles move faster than tense and tight ones. Our minds work the same way. Fill it up with bad thoughts and you are killing your chances of success. Lastly, the hitter must use positive self-talk and affirmation statements. You could do the first two parts of the routine, but then get into the batter's box and say, "Don't chase the high fastball again." Remember, we go toward what we focus on. If a player does not master the last part of self-talk, then they are defeating the whole process and might as well go back to what they were doing before.

Pitcher Routine:

1. Focal Point = Shoelaces

2. Deep Breath = Get B.I.G. (Breath In Greatness)

3. Positive Self-Talk = Pound the zone, Hit the glove, etc.

Notice the self-talk is directed toward things the players can control. They are not saying get a hit or strike this guy out, which are two things they cannot control. We want the players to stay task/process-oriented and understand that once the ball hits their bat or leaves their hand, the rest is out of their control.

Fielding Routine:

1. Focal Point = Glove

2. Deep Breath = Get B.I.G. (Breathe In Greatness)

3. Positive Self-Talk = Feet on time, React

Again, understand that the focal point needs to be something simple that will be at every field you play on. Some players like using the foul pole, shoelaces, their glove, home plate, batting gloves, the rubber, a rock on the mound—it does not matter, as long as they use it.

Action Steps:

1. Have your players create routines by writing them down.

2. This creates a script for them to follow when they need to get "locked in."

3. Make sure the routines sound good and employ all three parts to the Pre-Pitch Routine.

4. Collect them and study what each hitter's routine is going to be. Know them and hold the players accountable when they do not follow their own routine, or have them step out of the box and re-commit to the routine. If you can recognize when a player is speeding things up, help them by using a mental cue from your own list like "Get B.I.G." or "Lock In" or one from their own routine they created. The following is a list of mental cues players can use to stay focused on process and not the outcome that can be used as part of a self-talk:

Mental Cues Players Can Use

- SEE IT, HIT IT
- TRACK IT AND WHACK IT
- GET B.I.G.
- SEE BALL, HIT BALL
- POUND THE MITT
- SEE THE GLOVE
- GET LOCKED IN
- FOCUS
- FLUSH IT
- CLEAR IT
- GET TOUGH
- BE IN THE GREEN
- I WANT THE BALL
- BELIEVE IN YOURSELF
- TRUST YOURSELF
- I AM PREPARED
- I AM READY
- MOVE ON
- W.I.N.

- A.C.E.

- B.A.T. PROGRAM

- STAY IN THE GREEN

- THIS PITCH, THIS MOMENT

- ONE-PITCH-AT-A-TIME

- BE IN THE PRESENT MOMENT

- FAKE IT, TIL YOU MAKE IT

- JUST DO IT

- SPEND THE DOLLAR

- JUST REACT

- TRUST MY STUFF

- I CAN DO THIS

- IT'S OVER, LET'S MOVE ON

- CONTROL MY A.P.E.

- BE A FOUNTAIN

- RELEASE YOUR MENTAL BRICKS

- COMPARED TO WHAT?

- DEAL WITH IT

- CONTROL WHAT YOU CAN

- ACT AS IF

- WORK YOUR PLAN

- 2 X 4
- CLEAR THE WATER
- THE TIME IS NOW
- NO PINK ELEPHANTS
- SEE IT HAPPENING
- BE ON TIME
- NO STINKIN' THINKIN'
- DEEP BREATH
- GET FOCUSED
- BE A BULLDOG
- TRUE BLUE
- BATTLE
- WIN THIS PITCH
- DRIVE IT
- GOOD CONTACT
- GET A GOOD JUMP
- RELEASE IT
- LETS REFOCUS
- A.T.W.
- WHAT DO IT WANT

- ATTACK IT AND SMACK IT
- FORGET ABOUT IT
- SO WHAT
- KEEP IT IN PERSPECTIVE
- STICK TO THE PROCESS
- KEEP A GOOD PERSPECTIVE
- RELAX
- KEEP IT SIMPLE
- NO PRESSURE
- SMILE
- HAVE FUN
- PLAN, PREPARE, PERFORM
- POUND THE ZONE
- GET A STRIKE
- PLAY THE BALL
- ZONE IN
- RIGHT TO THE GLOVE
- RIGHT TO HIS CHEST

50. CREATE A *1PITCH WARRIOR* VOCABULARY

The thing that has made a huge difference is creating terminology that is short, concise, and that everyone can understand. As coaches, we do not have the time during the game to tell a player to do his routine and to take a deep breath and focus when they are in the middle of an at-bat. It just is not realistic, but you can have a go-to saying like "Get B.I.G." or "Lock It In." You can base your Skull Session around teaching your players about terms you feel are important within your program. Whether it is Brian Cain's "So What, Next Pitch" Mentality, or one you develop yourself, language is a vital part of creating a program of excellence getting everyone on the same page.

51. RELEASE ROUTINES

We have already talked about the importance of game routines to play the game pitch-by-pitch and focused. Other routines I like each player to have in his mental toolbox are to release the bad at-bat, the error they just made, or the homerun they gave up. I think these are crucial moments in a game when a player needs to understand that success in the future may be directly linked to his ability to handle the adversity the game has just thrown in his way. If he is able to use a release routine to get back to playing the game in the present moment, then he has given himself the best chance for success in his next opportunity to hit, pitch, make a play, etc.

Some examples of these release routines, which are different than the regular pre-pitch routine:

1. A player strikes out and does not take off his batting gloves or puts his helmet back in the helmet rack until he releases the bad and is ready to play the next pitch. Often times this never happens. The player comes into the dugout, taking off his gloves in a fury, tosses the helmet down without slamming it, but one can certainly tell he is not happy about

things. Which is fine, he should not be. But responding is different than reacting to what just happened. He does this because he does not have the "go-to routine" or the know-how. He has not been trained well. We are not talking about something that players of any ability or age level cannot do. It is easy, as long as there is a script for them to use.

2. Another example is a pitcher who gives up a homerun, jumps back on the mound and starts trying too hard to get the next hitter, only to eventually walk the batter. I feel much more confident when I see a pitcher give up the bomb, take a walkabout behind the mound, focus on something in the outfield, take that deep breath, then go back to work. It might seem insignificant, but it is huge if the player can center himself once again and get back to work with a clear head about committing to throwing strikes and not trying too hard. Remember, working hard at the wrong things does not work.

Have your players write their release routines, as well. We want to develop a script for when the ump says, "Play ball," much like an actor has a movie script to go by once the director says, "Action." Let them be creative with it. Pick up dirt, squeeze the dirt, throw it down, release the bad play, and move on to the next pitch. I want to remind you that the release routine must be something physical that they can do, not just something they are going to say to themselves.

52. BRICKS

Another thing we use in our dugout is a brick inscribed with the phrase "Flush It." We use it as reminder for players to leave the mental brick behind and not take it out with them into the field. Of course players are going to say that they would not want to field a groundball or fly ball with a brick in their back pocket, but that is what it feels like when you carry that poor play into the field. Let your players hold the brick. Let them feel the weight of it. Their negative thoughts also feel this way. They bring them down, slow them down, and give them the loser limp. The power is within their own heads to rid themselves of the mental brick and play as a *1-Pitch Warrior.*

The brick sits right on the bat rack when we are at a home game and we do not leave without it for an away game. There were a few times we forgot it and had to turn the bus around to get it. Never leave home without it. If the *1-Pitch Warrior* Mentality is something you want to advertise to your players, the brick is an essential piece of the puzzle to create a program that knows mental toughness is a necessary tool for excellence.

53. MENTAL TRAINING DAILY

Let's face it. You only get so much time with your team every day. The best coaches find ways for their players to continue to get better even away from the field. Working on mental toughness outside the confines of the field is certainly possible. I give my players things to work on daily— things that they do not like to do or some things they might skip. They are easy tasks that everyone can finish, but sometimes is the thing we just do not want to do. Mental toughness is about being able to do the things you do not want to do when you do not want to do them. Training ourselves to do easy mundane tasks can help with this once it comes to bigger and more important things.

Here is a list of things you can have your team do daily:

1. Make his bed immediately to start the day. This says he is ready to pay attention to detail and may be something he

never does, for one reason or another. The reasons are not important; acting differently than how you feel is the point of the activity.

2. Brush his teeth two times daily, no matter how late he is up and wants to go to bed.

3. No texting and driving.

4. Buckle up every time he is in a car, no matter the distance.

Other ideas might be to read a small part of a book every morning, watch inspirational videos daily, or keep a journal.

Visit www.1pitchwarrior.com/free
for the BONUS *1-Pitch Warrior*
9 "Innings" of Free *1PW* Training Resources!

NOTES:

Justin Dehmer

IDEAS TO BUILD YOUR PROGRAM

The challenge for great coaches is to not only to build a competitive product on the field, but also to get the community involved and a part of the program well into the future. What I have discovered is that programs with amazing traditions are completely devoted to the program as a whole, not just the varsity or JV. If it is to become a program of excellence for years, it will be relentlessly dedicated to the youth. They are the future of your program. To build a respected program, there are many things that can be done within the community to get your program involved in projects outside of the game of baseball.

54. BATBOY/GIRL

As a coach, I was always looking for ways to get the community involved in our program and, most importantly, get the youth involved, knowing they were the future of our program. I did the obvious camps and clinics that most programs do, but I wanted to try to do something different, too. During our home games, we would have an honorary batboy for each game. We put out the season schedule on the school's website and asked any youth from the community to sign-up for nights that would work for them. We limited it to one night per player.

Basically, the batboy becomes another member of the team. We announce him as part of the team, and give him a t-shirt to keep. He lines up with us for the anthem and helps out in whatever way we need during the game. After the game is over, the batboy comes out with us to break it down and leads us in a loud, victorious "DEVILS!" Players really like it. I get countless emails from parents telling me how much fun their son had and how he will not stop talking about it. The main point is to get kids interested in playing baseball and, instead of just watching how much fun we have, to actually be part of it. I want them to have a lasting impression of what it means to be a Blue Devil and plant that seed early so that he goes home saying, "I can't wait to play baseball as a Blue Devil." This is how our traditions can carry us on.

I have to say that it works so well that we had to up it to two batboys per game after doing it for a few years. Once the post-season rolled around, we usually stuck with one of the batboys—you undoubtedly know how superstitious baseball players and coaches can be. In any event, I highly recommend you give it a try if you are not already doing something like this in your program.

55. CAMPS

Obviously having camps are an essential part of building any solid program and a way to give back to the community. We do this in a variety of ways from year to year. Sometimes we have a three- to four-day camp over spring break; sometimes we have a winter camp; a spring camp outdoors; sometimes it is a weekend camp that runs for four weeks. How you do it is up to you, but not taking the chance to interact with the future of your program is robbing your program of its future.

The things I try to accomplish with the camps are:

1. Get as many players to the camp as possible. We are a small school so we want to try to get 100% of the younger players there, from third grade up to eighth grade. This means making it affordable to all families. I do not want to make it into a fundraiser. It is a camp for which we charge a tiny amount. I do not want money to be a factor in why someone

does not show up. In addition, I have to try to get dates that work for people. Spring Break Camp had to go, because too many families were out of town. I get the word out through fliers to the elementary school parents, an ad on the school website, contacting the local Little League, and using social media.

2. Another thing that can work great is if you have your older players work the camps with you. The younger players really look up to the players in your program, even more so sometimes than they do you. Give your players the chance to experience what coaching is like. Some may find that they like coaching and may pursue it as a profession. I know a few from our program have. This also forces players to think differently about the game and really helps, not only the youngsters to learn the game, but also your older players. They will gain a better perspective for what it is like to be a coach and the difficulties that go along with teaching the game to kids.

3. Obviously the knowledge passed along was huge, as well. Planting those seeds of success at an early age is so important.

4. I also encouraged parents to stay for the entire camp. I want them to ask questions and be curious about what they can do at home to help. They will have more contact with their son or daughter than we will throughout the year, so equipping them with the knowledge to continue fostering growth and development is vital for our program. We have had many dedicated moms and dads in our program who have helped their sons get better. It is a big piece that should never be overlooked.

56. VOLUNTEER – COMMUNITY SERVICE

We want to make a difference to our players on the field, but often we get so wrapped up in making our team better, that we forget that we can make a difference in the community, too. I encourage you to set aside a day during the practice season to work to make an impact within a part of your school district. I am not saying to cut out practice completely that day, but maybe once it is over, you volunteer at a homeless shelter, a food bank, for the Special Olympics, do random yard work for older people in the community, or some type of project that may benefit the school itself.

I know many teams in the Des Moines area that help out with an organization called The Miracle League, which helps children with disabilities play an actual game of baseball. It is an awesome sight to see and I know that your team will get much out of it, if they ever have a chance to do something similar in your area. We talk so much about having a great perspective and the Compared to What? mentality that we want to ingrain in our players. This is a great example of when you help others, you will get better, too.

57. CARNIVAL/COMMUNITY NIGHT

One great idea that I took from a coach was a carnival night. I personally never tried it because of the size of town I coached in, but I think for bigger schools this could be something worth giving a try. Anyway, to get people to the game and to see your program in action is always a great idea, in my mind.

Not only is it going to bring the youth of your community to the field, but also it is a potential fundraiser and something that everyone in your area can learn to look forward to each year.

Make it as big, or as small as you want, but I think it could become a great tradition.

58. SENIOR NIGHT

Every program does a senior night to honor its players who will be moving on to new things after graduation. This is pretty much a given. How it is organized varies from program to program. We always have our senior night on the same night as the Little League Night so that we have more people there at the game. Also, we want the youth of our program to look up to and see the seniors.

Ideas to make a nice senior night:

1. Have flowers for the moms

2. Write up a personal short story about each player

3. Do not bog it down with stats; people will not remember them

4. Include a favorite moment while in your program

5. Have their future plans included

6. Make sure to take lots of pictures

7. My favorite: have your seniors pick someone they admire to throw out the first pitch. You could vary this by having parents throw out the first pitch, or have players pick their favorite teacher, instead. It is up to you, but no matter how you choose to do it, it is a pretty cool way to honor the support your seniors have received.

59. LITTLE LEAGUE NIGHT

Coupled with our Senior Night, we get as many players from our Little League to come to one of our last home games. Usually, it is the second to last game; just in case of rain, we have one other date open. The idea has always been to honor those players and their families who have made their way through our program. It is also a way to honor the future players—players we want wearing the Blue Devil uniform four, five, six years from now. It has always gone really well.

The current players make a tunnel for the younger kids and give them high fives as they go through the tunnel. The kids get excited that the older players are there to encourage them and that they get to come out onto the field. Parents appreciate the night and we make sure to honor the coaches who volunteer their time for the teams. We announce the Little League first, leave them on the field, and then announce the seniors. Building ties within the community is a big part of a head coach's job that often goes overlooked. Whether it is a night like Little League night, having a little coach's clinic, camps, or parent clinics, traditions are created when there is a sense of belonging to something bigger than one's self.

The one other thing we do that night is let everyone into the game for free. We want everyone to come and be part of the Blue Devil Tradition. Little Leaguers are encouraged to wear their uniforms.

60. MVP JERSEY

One thing we do every season during our team award ceremony/ banquet at the end of the year is award an MVP. The way this is done is, throughout the year each night, a player is selected to be the practice or that game's Most Valuable Player. The part that I really like about this is the players are responsible for awarding the jersey to the next MVP. So, if I was the MVP at Monday's practice and we have a game Tuesday, I would know that I am going to have to give it out and have a good reason for it. This way a player can never get the MVP jersey two nights in a row.

The only time coaches give it out is the very first time. Usually, it is given out at the first pre-season meeting, or at the very first practice. If we happen to give it out at the pre-season meeting, it may be to the player who has been to the most off-season workouts honoring his commitment to improving himself. If it is the first practice, I like picking a player who hustled and showed the type of tenacity it takes to be a champion.

The jersey is exactly that—a uniform that is a one-of-a-kind design, different from any of our other jerseys. We get a new one made every season. The player who was awarded the jersey the day before, wears the jersey to practice, or BP if we have a game. We want him to be proud of earning it.

As a coach, I just record the times each player is awarded the jersey in a spreadsheet. At the end of the year, I will know who is the MVP of our team and that player will be given the jersey at our end of the year get-together.

61. MORE IDEAS ON RECOGNIZING PLAYERS

A few other ideas to motivate and recognize your players for their efforts on and off the field are:

1. Tour de Fense shirt – They give out the yellow jersey at the Tour de France and you can give out the Tour de Fense when a player comes up big defensively and makes a play

that saves a game. This is not something that you give out every night, but you could if you want to. Players would know when a teammate has made a play worthy of earning the t-shirt. Get some made up before the season with your team's logo and a saying on the front. It will undoubtedly be something that players will wear for years to come.

2. *1-Pitch Warrior* Shirt – Give out the shirt when a player has overcome some adversity— battled his way through things only to come out tougher and more mentally prepared than ever before. Recognizing players for this will only help create more mentally tough players in your program. Again, it does not have to be given out every day or every game, but the opportunity to earn it will be. If you are interested in ordering any shirts with the *1-Pitch Warrior* logo on it, please email me at coachd@1pitchwarrior.com.

3. GPA (Great Player Average) – I know some programs have giveaways for players who, not only excel on the field, but also off the field. The types of players that every coach wants are the ones who do their best in all aspects of life, not just at practice. Anything you can do to honor those types of players will go far to create more of them in your program.

4. Attendance – You can give away some sort of hoodie, pullover, or shirt for players who are in attendance for your pre-season pitcher/catcher workouts, lifting, and agility workouts. Make it whatever percent you want, but follow through with them and make them earn it.

62. SOCIAL MEDIA

If you have not jumped on the social media bandwagon yet, I think you are missing out. Having a Twitter account and a Facebook page set up for your team can have many benefits and are not hard to do and manage, even for those who are not tech-savvy. Once set up, all of the postings can be done directly from your smart phone. There are many services out there that allow you to post the same message to both Twitter and Facebook.

A few of the benefits:

1. Your players use this, so why not you. This allows you to communicate to them via their preferred platform.

2. Your program becomes more accessible and visible to the community.

3. You can use it to communicate with parents and the broader community.

4. It allows you to highlight your team and player accomplishments. It is another way to recognize performances on a nightly basis, plus lets people know how the team faired every single game of the season. This is also great for a player's relatives who live far away.

5. It helps creates an online community of future, current, and past players from your program.

6. It can be used to send out motivational messages and help create the type culture you want to build within your program.

63. POST ACCOMPLISHMENTS/UPDATE RECORDS

If you want to create tradition, you need to start by honoring the accomplishments of your current players, but also acknowledge the great seasons played by other teams and individuals from the past. Post these records to your Facebook page, or if you happen to have a team website, posting it there may be even more appropriate. This is a tedious task, especially if it has been neglected for a while. However, it will be worth it once it is done.

You can use this to help create a sense of accomplishment for your team and highlight the goals for the team and individuals to shoot for.

Ideas for your records:

Pitching Records to keep

Wins for career and a single season

Innings pitched for career and a single season

Strikeouts for career, a single season, and a single game

Fewest Walks for career (minimum 100 innings pitched) and a single season (minimum 50 IP)

Earned Run Average for career and a single season

Undefeated Seasons

Saves for career and a single season

Complete Games for career and a single season

Shut Outs for career and a single season

Games Pitched for career and a single season

Offensive Records to keep

Batting Average for career and a single season

Runs Batted In for career, a single season, and a single game

Hits for career, a single season, and a single game

Doubles for career, a single season, and a single game

Triples for career, a single season, and a single game

Home runs for career, a single season, and a single game

Runs Scored for career, a single season, and a single game

Hit by Pitch for career, a single season, and a single game

Games Played for career

At-Bats for career, a single season, and a single game

Stolen Bases for career, a single season, and a single game

Base on Balls for career, a single season, and a single game

Sacrifices for career, a single season, and a single game

Team Records to Keep

Wins in a Season, Conference Wins, Longest Winning Streak, Most Home Wins, Most Road Wins, Runs in a Game, Runs in an Inning, Hits in a Game, Hits in an Inning, Doubles in a Game, Home Runs in a Game, Stolen Bases in a Game, Largest Margin of Victory

Team Records for a Season—Batting Averages, Home Runs, RBIs, Hits, Doubles, Triples, Stolen Bases, Runs Scored, Walks, Sacrifices, At-Bats, Hit by Pitches

Team Pitching Records for a Season—Wins, ERA, Innings Pitched, Strikeouts, Fewest Walks, Saves, Complete Games, Shut Outs

Team Defensive Records—Put-Outs, Assists, Fielding Percentage

Post-Season Accomplishments—Conference Champs, District Champs, State Tournament Appearances, State Championships

I highly recommend you honor those last few in a special way, by placing the years that the team was able to accomplish them, in the dugout or outfield.

64. GIVE OUT DISTINCTIVE AWARDS AT THE END OF THE YEAR

Every program does an awards night, but I wanted to try to do something a bit different by doing unique awards. We create a document that looks official and give it to the player we feel either best represented that award or earned it through his play. Some of the awards we give out are: Base Thief, Batting Champion, Charlie Hustle, Coach's Award, Defensive Player of the Year, Gold Glove Infield, Gold Glove Outfield, Leadership and Commitment, Most Improved Player, Mr. True Blue, Mr. Utility, MVP, Offensive Player of the Year, and Pitcher of the Year.

We give these awards to not only the varsity but also the JV.

65. WINNING STARTS BEFORE THE GAME STARTS

There were always four things we were trying to win before the game ever started. They were Batting Practice, Warm-Ups, Pre-Game Infield/Outfield, and the National Anthem.

During batting practice, we do not stop hitting or at times taking groundballs until the other team shows up at our home games. We wait for them to get into the dugout so that they can watch us do a couple of things. One, we use our ATEC Rookie Machine to shoot fly balls as high as possible to our catchers and they catch them. These are towering fly balls that travel much farther than any player would ever hit during the game. It is good for the catchers, for obvious reasons, but it is also a technique I use to try to intimidate the other team. We want them to see how prepared we are and it sucks them into our world. If we can get them to watch us, it takes their focus away and distracts them.

The second thing we would do is tear down the field as fast as possible after batting practice. We huddle together, give a 1, 2, 3...Devils! Every player has a job to do as well—dismantle screens, take off mats, run off L-Screens, buckets, etc. It is always done for time and hustle is a must. The other team usually is amazed at what they are watching. They are probably thinking, "Who tears down the field while on a sprint. These guys are crazy. How are we going to beat them?" I want to set a tone of excellence before the game ever starts, and also show the other team our level of commitment excellence. Even with the most mundane tasks that most teams all do the same, I see an opportunity to be different.

The third thing we try to win before the game started is the comparison between our stretching, warm-ups, and pre-game infield/outfield and theirs. I want our team to be exactly that—a team. We are a group working together to put its best foot forward with all tasks, even the ones that do not seem as important as others. There are no little things! We always want a clean looking infield-outfield that had tempo and energy. We show the other team that we can catch and throw with the best of them.

The last thing we win before every game is the National Anthem. Every year we have a certain way we are going to stand as a team. Everyone stands this way, without moving, once the Anthem starts and stays that way until the song is over, plus a count to three. If you watch most teams carefully, you will see that every player is doing his own thing—standing differently, possibly moving, talking, going back to the dugout before the Anthem is over, or any number of other things. What does this say about your team if everyone is doing his own thing? I love attention to detail and I feel it is a key element in what separates excellence from mediocrity. Develop a system to honor the National Anthem and your team at the same time. Have your players decide how the team will stand and take ownership of it. Practice it! I have the team do this every day before we start stretching and warming-up.

66. CREATE A POSTER WITH A SCHEUDLE

One thing that can get community involvement and support from your local businesses is a team poster with the schedule on it. You can ask businesses in your area to put them up in their windows, have teachers put them up in their classrooms, and hand some out at your first few home games.

If you want to take it a step further, you can use it as a fundraiser and ask businesses to contribute a certain fee to be a sponsor of your program. Put their logos or business cards on the poster as a sponsor. Once the poster is created and printed, have the players sign an extra poster to give to the sponsors as a thank you.

As for the picture, it seems on every team there is always a mom or dad who is good at photography and can take and edit the picture for the final product. I know many teams do some sort of slogan in conjunction with a cool photo in front of something like a fire truck, construction zone, classroom, etc. This is something different you can do to highlight your team and ultimately get people to your games by advertising your program in your community.

67. PLAYER PACKET – WHAT ARE YOUR NON-NEGOTIABLES?

The following is a page from my player packet describing the qualities that we want our players to possess and attain by the time they leave the program.

MSTM BLUE DEVIL BASEBALL

"True Blue"

Respects the game, the team, and himself.

*Is determined to succeed on the field
and in the classroom.*

*Controls the tempo of the game
by being in control of himself.*

*Plays the game one-pitch-at-a-time
with the Awareness To Win.*

*Works hard on and off the field,
especially when no one is watching.*

*Accepts responsibility for his own actions,
as well as those of the team.*

*Works hard and smart to get better every day,
both mentally and physically.*

*Leads by example, commands respect
through his actions and work habits.*

*Will not except anything but an all-out effort
from himself and his teammates.*

*Is a passionate student of the game and strives
to gain inexpensive experience.*

*Lives in the present moment, focused on the process,
and in a positive mindset.*

*Leaves every last ounce of energy on the field,
playing as if today is his last.*

*Lives in the blood, sweat, and tears, no excuses,
no regrets, plays like a champion.*

*Shows tremendous pride in being a Blue Devil,
by fully committing to the team concept.*

*Sets aside individual differences off the field
and commits to being a brother on the field.*

*The strength of the Blue Devils
is in the individual.
The strength of the Blue Devil is in the team.*

*Has a hard-nose attitude, a positive mindset,
a championship swagger,
and big league confidence.*

Toughness, Every pitch, Attitude, Matters

I have the "True Blue" page first, after a cover page to remind players about the type of season we want to have. Then, comes my "Contract" page with the rules that players are to follow. I only have a set of five rules along with five consequences if the rules are broken. Not a long list. I feel that a short list is practical and easy enough to remember for players and me. Here is an example of the Contract:

TRUE BLUE/P.R.I.D.E. Contract

I am fully aware that great teams and great programs do not come from extraordinary athletes. They come from athletes who have extraordinary determination and an extraordinary work ethic. I am willing to do my part in the classroom and on the field to make this program better than it was the day before. I set the standard for my teammates and those who come after me to follow. I am here for the team and the team goals. My own success is secondary to what the team is working toward. I pledge to be "True Blue."

EXPECTATIONS:

1. I will be on time and in uniform (hat, belt, baseball pants, blue socks, blue or MSTM shirt tucked in, cleats on, hair cut and face shaved) ready to go when practice is scheduled. If I am not five minutes early, I am late.

2. Once I step on the field, there is never any walking; there is only hustle and hard work.

3. I will respect the game and will play the game the way it is supposed to be played. That includes things such as running out every hit, wearing my uniform correctly, and not disputing any calls from the umpires.

4. I will respect myself and others, on and off the field.

5. I will give everything that I have to try to make this season a masterpiece and reach the goals the team has set for this upcoming season.

CONSEQUENCES:

1. If you are missing a part of your proper practice or game attire you will have to go home to get it, or sit out of practice, or lose your starting spot for that game. Late players will have to complete 3 triangles under 1:30 before participating in anything. Missing practice without a call or explanation beforehand is a one-game suspension.

2. If you are not hustling, one of the coaches will ask you to sit out of practice for a specified time. If it continues, game time could be lost.

3. Throwing a helmet or bat, not running out a groundball, arguing a call, or saying something to an umpire that is disrespectful, will lead you to the bench. No exceptions.

4. Anything that is seen as disrespectful off the field could lead to running, missing games, or removal from the team.

5. All we ask for during practice or games is that you give 100% and represent your school, community, and teammates in the correct way.

Parent or Guardian Signature: _____

Player Signature: _____

Coach Signature: _____

As you can see there is a place for everyone to sign including me.

I give players a week to get the contracts signed and if they are not signed, I do not let them practice with the team. I feel the contract is important so that everyone would be on the same page and operate without any assumptions or misconceptions about what might happen if someone did get in trouble. It also makes it easy for me to follow exactly what was written if a situation did arise. I imagine most coaches have their own rules and I think it is interesting to hear how others do it, too. Modify what you have read here to fit your program and make it work.

68. HAVE A PARENT MEETING

In conjunction with having a player contract that everyone must sign is the all-important parent meeting. I think both are a must to get information out to parents about what to expect with your program. A couple things I suggest are to have your athletic director present at your parent meeting and also make sure he has a copy of your player packet. You need to make sure that if parents go to the athletic director behind your back, that he can defend you, understands where you are coming from, and what your expectations are. Having him or her there is a show of support for you and what you are trying to accomplish which can go a long way in stopping parents from whining to administration before anything ever starts.

Things to talk about during your parent meeting—

1. Go over rules again; give parents the opportunity to ask questions

2. Expectations

3. Playing Time at all levels

4. Contact info

5. Concessions

6. Order forms for gear

7. Fundraising Info

8. Thank them for coming and for their support

69. SEED-SCRIMMAGE

We always spend the last three days of practice holding a 3-game, inter-squad series. We split up the teams as fairly as possible and go after it for three straight days. The teams are competing against each other for a team dinner that the losers must serve to the winning team. Each player is paired with an opposing player, who they either serve or are served. The 3-game series takes place Thursday night, Friday night, and Saturday morning. Parents and community are welcome at all games, but before Friday night's game, I have parent meetings in the bleachers just before the game starts. It seems like a good way to get parents to attend your parent meeting because they not only get to listen to your talk, but also see the team play before the season starts. I always find that I have better attendance this way.

Along with the parent meeting (for which I send out email invites well in advance), we call the game that night the Seed Scrimmage. We ask anyone in attendance that night to bring a bag of seeds as admittance into the game. We collect bags and bags of seeds for our players. We keep them in the concession stand and get them out for players in the dugout. On away games, one of our coaches grabs a few bags for the games that night. We usually collect enough bags to last at least half a season. We even ask a mom make a seed bucket to pour the seeds into that is decorated in duck tape with our saying and motto for that year. Advertise, advertise, and advertise! Every little bit helps.

70. PLAYER WALL OF FAME

Once you have your records together, you can use them to create a Wall of Fame for your locker room, clubhouse, dugout, etc. Use the categories to recognize players who have done special things in your program. If you do not want to use the records, you can honor players who are All-Conference, All-District, All-State or all three. Anything you can do to inspire the youth of your program the better; always err on the side of giving too much recognition, rather than too little. Parents and players will appreciate it and, when they come back years later, they will still feel a part of something special. After all, who does not want to have his name up on a wall?

Visit www.1pitchwarrior.com/free
for the BONUS *1-Pitch Warrior*
9 "Innings" of Free *1PW* Training Resources!

NOTES:

WAYS TO BUILD TEAM UNITY

Talent is not the only requirement to win games. It takes much more than pure athletic ability to be a championship type of team. I believe that, much like mental toughness, team unity can be taught and, given the right opportunities, grow just like the mental game. The problem is most coaches do not invest the necessary time to help their players become one unit that will fight for each other. Most coaches think that the unity part will grow on its own. Sometimes it may, because players may already be good friends. In any event, it can certainly get better. There is always room for improvement. If a plant is not watered, it will grow by simple putting it outside. But, with dedicated attention, this plant can grow bigger and stronger, much like your team needs help to grow in team unity. Just because the players are together at practice does not mean that growing together will happen.

71. FUN COMPETITIVE GAMES

Earlier I mentioned how you can use competitive games during the course of practice to help your team become more competitive and give them a chance to get away from the traditional run-of-the-mill drills and skills parts of practice. You can do this same sort of thing to develop team unity off the field, too. Schedule a poker night, play charades, or Pictionary. Pick a game that everyone can be involved in. The more players laugh and have fun, the better. The more laughs the better. My challenge to you is to schedule a team night once a month to foster growth and build team unity.

72. KARAOKE NIGHT

Another fun thing to do is to get the players way out of their comfort zone by having them sing karaoke. For most players, this will be forcing them to act differently than they feel, but it is with their teammates and coaches. I go into it saying that everyone must perform at least one song, coaches included. Again, you could break up the team into a few different groups of varying ages. Make it competitive with the coaches serving as the judges. It is a fun way to get kids out of their shells and build team chemistry along with the type of comfort with each other that it takes to build champions.

73. TRUST FALL

Many people know what a trust fall is. There is a good chance that you or someone you know has been a part of a trust fall. It is a simple concept that used within the confines of a team is a great activity to do. Trust, especially in baseball and softball is a huge part of becoming a total team. Pitchers throw the ball over the plate knowing that, more than likely, it will be hit and they need to trust that the players behind them will play their roles making the routine plays and maybe even an outstanding one occasionally. Whether it is Tim Robbins and walking fire or Brian Cain eating fire, it takes a leap of faith to conquer the fear of falling or fire. It can be overcome by committing to the task at hand. The thing I like about the trust fall is you need your teammates to catch you. Walking across fire and eating fire are awesome things to do but are a one-person event. Plus, most schools and athletic directors may have a bit of an issue with the whole fire thing. The trust fall might be just as dangerous, but on the surface the fire seems a bit scarier.

Developing that trust and faith in your teammates through a trust fall can certainly be a team builder. I prefer the elevated version rather than just standing on the ground. The fall of faith can take place from a chair, ladder, stool, etc. Get the rest of the members of your team to alternate their arms, so that once the catch comes, the weight is distributed evenly. The person falling needs to cross his arms and keep his body straight like a plank as he falls backwards.

This could be a practice starter for you to do with one player at the beginning of practice, or something you do with your team at a pre-season meeting you might schedule every year. I do not think you will be disappointed. Chances are none of your players have ever done a trust fall so getting them out of their comfort zone will be good for them and the morale of the team, too.

74. WALK THE PLANK

Another team builder that is a great way to overcome fear and also let players understand that sometimes we make the situation bigger or more complicated than it really needs to be is a balance beam walk. The concept is simple. Place the beam or plank on the ground and have players walk across it. Hopefully, for most of your players, it is an easy task to accomplish and getting across is not a problem.

After they have all completed that walk, move the beam to the top of two chairs, or better yet, two ladders. The higher you go, the more pressure you will put on them—there was no pressure when the beam was on the ground. The team-building aspect comes in by having your players around the beam on both sides to catch anyone who may fall.

It is also a great activity to do with players to make sure they understand that the task does not change from the ground to up in the air. The beam is still the same width and the length. What does change is their perspective on the task—how it seems so much more difficult and they usually start to over analyze it. What if I fall? What if I don't make it? What if, what if, what if? We want to teach players to deal in the WHAT IS not the WHAT IF.

This is the same for situations during games. Nobody on, no outs, up seven runs—players tend to be relaxed. Down two with the bases loaded, and two outs in the bottom of the seventh—players tend to be a bit tenser. The question why? The task is the same. See ball, hit ball hard. The problem lies in the fact that players allow the situation to become bigger than it needs to be and they focus on the situation instead of focusing on what is. What If? means you are focusing on something beyond the future. What Is means you are ready to dominate the present moment and do what you can on this pitch.

Once the players try the elevated beam, have them focus on the What Is. They just did the same task ten minutes before and it has not changed, nor should their focus.

75. SHARE - PERSPECTIVE POSTERS

Earlier I discussed making perspective posters with your players and having them create one on their own. A great way to piggyback this activity is to have players share with everyone what is on their poster. To really know someone, means you have to understand what makes him tick and also what disappointments he has faced in life or is currently going through. Getting players to know each other on this type of level is good team building. It is also a great way for your players to get to know your coaching staff on a more personal level. Too often I think there lies a gap between players and coaches. Coaches who open themselves up to their players allow players to gain an insight they might not otherwise attain. After all, it is said that players do not care how much you know, until they know how much you care.

76. HAVE A TEAM HANDSHAKE

Players see it all the time on ESPN; every MLB team seemingly has a team handshake. Each is as unique as the players who use them. Sometimes during the year, the handshake takes on a life of its own and that becomes the team's way of identifying big moments, great plays, and sending congratulations to each other. What if, instead of magically hoping it happens on its own, you ask your team leaders come up with their own forearm shiver or fist pound? It could certainly be a copy or adaptation of something they have seen before from another team or on TV. But one thing is certain, and that is it should be different than last year's. Every year is different, and no matter how good last season was, this team is new and it deserves its own identity. Have your leaders introduce it to your other players, or you could make it an exercise for the entire team, not just your upperclassmen.

77. ALUMNI GAME

What better way to create a sense of pride and respect for your program than to get alumni back to play a game against your current players. Some baseball teams host an actual baseball game, others do a slow-pitch softball game. The same could be true for softball teams. The point is having players come back after they have been through your program—it is a great way to blend the current tradition with the old. At first, it may start slowly, but stick with it and it will become an event players will enjoy and really look forward to. It also gives old players the chance to see the upgrades you have made to your facilities. As a fundraising tool, it is a way to show them where the money is going or a way to show them firsthand the needs of your program. So, if you use the alumni game as a way to raise money for a certain item(s), they know it will be well spent.

78. OTHER IDEAS FOR TEAM BUILDING

We already discussed some ideas on ways to foster your players' growth together helping them develop chemistry rather than expecting it to happen on its own. Here are a few other ideas you can try in conjunction with the others. Pick your favorites and use them throughout the year. Team chemistry is not a one-and-done type of thing. You must continually work at it to grow stronger and stronger.

Blind Numerical Order

Illustrates: Communication and listening.

1. There is no talking

2. You must keep your blindfolds on at all times

3. Each of you will have a number whispered into your ear

4. The goal is for the group to arrange itself in numerical order without speaking and without the use of sight

Blindfold all the participants. Whisper a number to each of them but do not allow other participants to hear. The number should be RANDOM—not just 1-12, etc. For a few participants, use negative numbers, "0", very high numbers, etc. After whispering the number, move the participant to a random location. Once every participant has a number, they should begin. Make sure all participants are safe throughout the exercise.

Some participants can be restricted even more by not allowing them to use their right arm, or left arm, etc.

Processing Questions—What was the most difficult aspect of this exercise? Did you have a sense of working together? Why or why not? How frustrating was it when you could not talk? What was necessary in order for you to be successful? Did you assume that the assigned numbers would be in order (like 1-12)? How important is good communication in groups? How does this activity relate to our group?

Board of Directors

Draw on a piece of paper a table with chairs. Participants write the names of the people who they would like to have as their board of directors (e.g., family members, teachers, friends, coaches, etc.). Participants share their list of mentors and why those people are important to them.

Human Knot

Participants should stand shoulder to shoulder in a circle. Each person should put his right hand into the middle of the circle and join hands with someone across the circle and not directly to his right or left. Each person then places his left hand into the circle and joins hands with a different person, and not the person directly to his left or right.

When the participants have their hands tangled, inform them they need to be untangled without ever breaking grips within the group. Note that there are three possible solutions: a circle, two interlocking circles, or two circles with a knot in it. Participants should not make sudden or large movements since they are all connected.

Processing questions—Was this challenging? Why? Or, why not?

How did the group approach this task? What was done effectively? What could have been done more effectively?

What role did you personally take in this exercise? How could each of you have increased participation in this activity? How can you relate your freshman experience to this activity?

Visit www.1pitchwarrior.com/free
for the BONUS *1-Pitch Warrior*
9 "Innings" of Free *1PW* Training Resources!

NOTES:

NOTES:

www.1pitchwarrior.com

NOTES:

FAVORITE DRILLS AND TEACHING AIDS

Every coach has their "go to" practice drills, teaching techniques, and teaching aids. I want to share my favorites for you to add to your practice plans and to implement at your next practice. I hope you find many of these resources helpful for your program and find success and excellence with them, as well.

79. BLACK AND WHITE BALL

One of the most undervalued parts of a player's game is how he throws the ball. Very little instruction is done in this area. I always see teams sent out to do their pre-game routine or pre-practice routine while the coaches are off doing their own thing. Coaches may be getting the field ready, visiting with each other in the dugout, chatting with the opposing coach, or doing other tasks that coaches have. Meanwhile, players are throwing and getting loose for practice. They may be developing bad habits, not working on good mechanics, or just going through the motions without any instruction or any feedback.

One easy way to give them immediate feedback is to color a ball black on one side when players have a four-seam grip. If players have a four-seam grip, one finger will be on white and the other finger will be on black. Once they throw the ball, they will know if they are getting the type of rotation needed for carry and good one-hops. Obviously, we look for the ball to stay white on one side and black on the other. If they cannot do this, then there is a breakdown in their mechanics, grip, or a combination of the two. I think this part of the game is often taken for granted. I make the players use the ball every day at practice and before games. I keep the balls in a long tube sock and the only time those balls get used is during pre-practice/pre-game. When done, they go right back in the sock. I even have our starting pitcher use the black and white ball for the first five to ten pitches in the bullpen.

Another way you can use the black and white ball is for rotation on a curve ball. If pitchers get their grip right on the horseshoe, then when they pull down on the seams, the rotation of a good curveball should also be black on one side and white on the other. We look for tight rotation and increasing the number of spins on the ball. This is great immediate feedback for pitchers on every pitch.

When you start your pre-season work, I do not have pitchers or players throw a ball without using the black and white ball. This is a fantastic way to teach young players to understand the type of rotation we need. No matter what position they play, all should be making throws with a four-seam grip.

80. STRIP AND RIP

This is one of the hitting drills we do on a daily basis that players love. I have used this with our guys and at clinics across the country. All the players love the way it makes them feel after they are done.

For the first four to five swings, players will use a doughnut on their bat. You can do it differently, but usually we have a coach or a player sitting on a bucket throwing underhand at a short distance behind an L-Screen. After the first round of swings with the doughnut on, players "Strip and Rip" on the last four to five swings. With the weight on, we look just for good bat path and solid contact. We want players to square up to the ball as many times as possible with swings that are between 75% to 90% of their maximum effort. The player then takes off the doughnut and goes all out. The hitter will feel like they have amazing bat speed and can crush the ball. They will have to wait for the ball to get deep in the zone and then explode, since the weight is now off, but we have had great feedback from our players and they are ultimately the ones who need to buy into the drills we do.

81. WEIGHTED BALLS

Another teaching tool that works in the same way as "Strip and Rip" is using weighted balls during a short toss. Either an underhand or overhand short toss is used on this drill. The balls I own are called Total Control Balls. They come in baseball and softball sizes and in different weights. I really like them for a few reasons:

1. It is just a different feel for hitter. Anything out of the ordinary that players have to do, I feel is a good thing. We want the drill to challenge them to think and hit outside their comfort range.

2. The balls are heavy, so players must drive through the ball to hit it with any type of pop. Even if they square up to it but do not drive through contact, the ball goes nowhere. This is immediate feedback for the hitter and coach.

3. We do four to five weighted balls first and then pitch regular balls at the end. I always like to end with a regular bat and regular balls on these drills, which I think allows the player to gain a feel for a quick swing and extra pop leading to confidence and an extra swagger come game time.

82. NO BATTING PRACTICE ON THE FIELD

This is one I can guarantee your players will not like, but it is for their own good. Most teams do take their batting practice on the field. It is almost a given and just one of those things that has always been the way it is done. I always try to challenge the thought or saying, "This is the way we always have done it." I look for new ways to practice, or at least be satisfied that the current ways are getting the job done.

I cannot say this for all players or teams, but I feel that once that first homerun is hit during BP, all players are trying to get the next one and it becomes some sort of homerun derby. To alleviate this problem, we did not hit on the field during our two undefeated seasons. We hit mainly in the cages, did our defensive work on the field, and swings were taken in the cage. I have yet to see a homerun in the cage and I think it helped our players focus much more on the mechanics and good solid preparation instead of seeing how far they could hit the ball on the field.

I use batting practice as more of a reward system than a right. We do allow them to hit on the field twice, but only as a reward for a great week, and never before a big game or post-season game. The one thing we do on the field is bunt at home, but other than that, defense is our main focus on the field. We split up the team. Outfielders hit in the cages and the infielders get their drill work on the field. Then we switch. It just makes sense to me to spend the hour before the game on both aspects of the game. I think most teams use that hour to hit, hit, and hit some more, with very little emphasis on defense other than the balls off the bat or the occasional fungo to an infielder. How many games did you lose last season because of a defensive miscommunication, error, or mental mistake? How you invest your time during BP may need an overhaul.

83. PRE-GAME INFIELD ROUTINE

During our batting practice sessions, this is the infield routine I typically run my infielders through:

Infield Daily Work – Game Day Routine

1. **Ready Position** – Dry runs x 5
   a. Working on bending back, one step toward home (either foot), then hop, landing on both feet simultaneously

2. **Short Hops with partner**
   a. Reinforce good fielding position; wide base, knees & back bent; hands out front
      i. Routine short hops x 10
      ii. Routine backhands x 10

3. **Knees Drill** x 5
   a. Get players in an arc around coach 20-25 feet away, hitting firm fungo to players right and left working on catching it out front and funneling it in

4. **Wide Base Drill** x 5
   a. Hard ground balls hit right at infielders, infielder takes five in a row working good base while funneling after catch, rapid fire

5. **Fungo behind mound** – Players need to time pre-pitch routine accordingly
   a. Routine ground balls – one bucket
   b. Backhands – one bucket
      i. First half is starting rotated chest high palm to the sky keeping glove out front
      ii. Second half regular position
      iii. Coach always making sure there is no extra tapping,

slapping, curling of the hands

   c. Smashes – one bucket

      i. Hard hit where players need to create angles and not get caught flat footed, take drop step to create long hops or work through balls to create short hops

6. **Closed Eye Fungos** – One bucket

   a. Players must react now but with only one eye open, switching eyes every other time

7. **Slow rollers** - Players working on field left, throw right, transfer in the middle, keeping hand behind the baseball and not under it

   a. Ball in glove x 5

   b. Slow rollers x 5

   c. Dead Ball x 5

8. **Tags** – Thrown by coach 2 sets of 5

   a. Straddle the base, let the ball travel, tag hard, straight down and up showing the umpire

9. **Relays** – Thrown by a coach 2 sets of 5

   a. Move players around creating balls they have to come get and also go with, always making sure players are receiving balls as close to their body as possible, replace feet to create direction and momentum

84. PRE-GAME OUTFIELD ROUTINE

This is the outfield work we would do with our outfielders while the infielders are hitting in the cages. The first six are daily drills and then we mix in one or two of the last ones, as needed.

Outfield Daily Work – Game Day Routine

1. **One Step Drop Back**- Sprint forward catching a line drive throw. Open both directions.

2. **Three Step Drop Back**- Sprint forward catching a line drive throw. Open both directions.

3. **Routine Fly Ball** - Place two cones 10 yards apart, run around the far cone, turn around and catch the routine flyball, hold the catch for three seconds.

4. **Star Drill** – Start in the middle, drop step at a 45-degree angle right, catch the ball from the coach. Repeat back with your back left angle, then front left, front right, side to side. Challenge them.

5. **Wrong Shoulder** – Place two cones 10 yards apart, run to the cone, coach throws over the opposite shoulder, turn head (should lose sight of the ball), find the ball and catch it. Repeat other side.

6. **Over The Shoulder** – Place two cones 10 yards apart, run to the cone and either go at a 45-degree right or left and catch the flyball from coach.

Other Outfield Drills

1. **Communication** – Coach stands behind 2nd base and throws balls in the gaps and the players call each other off, or if you have one from home, with the Rookie ATEC machine.

2. **Relays** – Hitting the cut-off man, in the gap, from the fence, working on proper feet placement and getting rid of the ball quickly with accuracy.

3. **Fielding Ground Balls** – Left foot forward for right-handed throwers; opposite for lefties.

4. **Flyballs** – Hitting fungos.

5. **Rob Home Runs** – Throw or hit balls close to the fence.

85. WEIGHTED BATS

We have used weighted bats called PowerPipes (www. baseballhittingadvantage.com). As I mentioned earlier, I am a big proponent of having players swing other bats instead of just a regular size bat all the time. Overloading with the PowerPipes has been a great training aid for our players. We have various sizes we use for different drills, but using a heavier bat makes it more difficult to swing and forces you to have good swing plane, not to mention that they are much narrower than a normal barrel. This means to square up to the ball becomes that much more difficult. When we use the PowerPipes, we always finish with our regular bat for at least three to four swings. We do all our regular drills with these bats to add a higher level of difficulty. Players like the feel of the PowerPipes. I had searched and searched for something like this, but never found anything that had the feel I was looking for. These bats have certainly helped with our overloading phase of the hitting process.

We do three swings with a really heavy bat, three swings a lighter PowerPipe, and then finish with our regular bat. We even use them with regularly thrown balls, not just soft-toss, short-toss, or a tee.

86. UNDERLOADING

Many teams utilize the overloading phase of hitting but I like to underload, too. I think it is a vital piece of building bat speed and better hand-eye coordination. Using fungos for tee work, soft-toss, or short-toss is a great way to start speeding up players' hands and to get that feel of great bat speed. I really like to alternate the underload and overload stations. We try to get as many swings with lighter bats as we do with the heavier bats.

Some example of stations might be a soft-toss station with the light bat or fungo. The next station would be a PowerPipe, or Strip and Rip underhand short toss. Always finish with the player's bat or a wood bat. We suggest that players use wood as much as possible. But, if they want to use their game bat the day of a game, that is not a problem. If it is not a game day, then it is no longer a suggestion. They use wood.

87. BASE RUNNING

Along with having a solid process for warming up and throwing, I feel that base running is another fundamental area that is either skimmed over, or not worked on enough. We do set time aside at the beginning of practice to work on all types of base running. When we do situations and other types of games on the field, base running is incorporated, too. This is so players, not only get the key fundamentals when we are setting aside time to teach it, but also are able to apply what they learn when we do situations. Just like with our defensive and offensive checklist, we use a base running checklist, too.

The things we work on are:

Getting down the line, touching front part of 1st base when running out a ground ball, finding the ball after touching 1st, rounding 1st base on a single, going over signs, doubles, triples, down angles at 3rd, hit and runs, straight steal, delayed steals, double steals, working a variety of looks and moves while working on steals from both righties and lefties, how we approach our lead-offs at 1st base, 2nd base, and 3rd base, secondary leads at 1st, 2nd, and 3rd, two out leads at 2nd base, when to tag at 2nd and 3rd, learning pitchers' tendencies, infield fly rule, squeeze, and double squeeze.

Those are the categories that I have on my offensive checklist. The number of times we go over each is entirely up to the type of team we have, but we will dedicate at least 15 minutes every day to take a handful of them to teach players what we expect.

We try to get two, three, or even four of the previously-listed base running techniques going at once. We might be working on rounds at 1st base while some guys are stealing at 1st and 2nd and working on reading down angle off the bat at 3rd. We mix it up and try to be as creative as possible. At times, we might even start extra lines at 1st and have three players stealing at the same time. Anything that allows more quality reps is always a good thing. If you have a great base running drill you do, or a sequence of things that works well for your program, please email me, as I would like to add coaches' ideas to a base running blog I am creating as a resource for others on my website www.1pitchwarrior.com. If you have not checked it out, you will find some good articles and a series of Championship Coaches Corner Blogs for your reading pleasure.

88. BASKETBALL DRILL

Another of my favorite hitting drills is using a basketball on a tee and having players work on driving through the ball. I like this drill because it really exposes a hitter's flaws in his swing. If they are getting around the basketball, it will be pounded into the ground as a rolled-over groundball to shortstop. If they are not driving through the ball, the rebound effect on their bat will come back toward them a bit.

We really try to get them to focus on hitting the inside of all pitches, but this drill puts a big-time emphasis on staying inside the ball and driving through the ball after contact. Because a basketball is bigger, heavier, and provides a different feel at contact than regular baseballs, players are working on staying short to the basketball and driving through the ball. I call it "short to it, long through it." Players must be strong at contact and extend through the force of basketball against the bat.

We do a few variations of this drill—

1. Straight up tee work

2. Happy Gilmore – Walk up and drive it. For a righty, the steps are a right crossover step in front of the left leg, loading up the backside and swinging. I like this drill, but you really need to watch players' bats and make sure they are not wrapping their bats around their heads, which players will have a tendency to do once they are trying to crush the basketball.

3. Soft-toss with the basketballs

4. Short-toss with the basketballs

89. LAY IT ON THE TOWEL

My favorite drill for bunting is a competition we have from time to time, with players learning how to bunt for a base hit. We lay a towel down on the field and players try to get the ball to stay on it. The idea is that, even if the slowest player we have, puts the ball on the towel, he is safe at 1st. We place towels on the 1st base line and also 3rd base line.

Our theory is that we want it perfect or foul if a player is trying to bunt for a hit. The worst thing we could do is have a terrible angle with our bat and bunt it to the pitcher who makes an easy out at 1st. The game is simple. Getting it on the towel wins a Gatorade or Mountain Dew. At times, we put the team into groups and they compete against each other for conditioning or no fieldwork rewards. Teams get five points if it lands on the towel and two points if it rolls or bounces over the towel. If the ball is bunted foul, it is one point. Zero points if it is a little off the line, and anything past that point, is minus one point. We set up cones so the players can see where the angles are. We want to reward players for doing what our philosophy is, which is perfect or foul. This is why they still get a point even if it is bunted foul. We still have an at-bat left and can make something happen rather than giving up an easy out.

90. EVERYONE BUNTS

One of my favorite bunting drills is having the team get one shot to get a bunt down for every player. Each bunter starts with a one ball, one strike count. This simulates a situation in which he may have already fouled a bunt off or had to take a pitch to let a runner steal a base and a strike was called. In other words, they have one chance to get the bunt down—added pressure to the bunter.

We do this after the team has worked on bunting in other drills, or have gone through rotations on the field while bunting at home. The idea is a simple one. Bunt or run. Every player must execute a bunt down one of the lines. Bunts back to the pitcher do not count. If everyone is able to do it, then they do not have to run. For every missed bunt, the entire team runs one triangle or some sort of conditioning. We put the cones out on the infield so players know what zones they are trying to bunt to and to make sure there is no question about in or out.

One of the fun things you can do here is to throw in a monkey wrench and see if players are willing to gamble. Tell them double or nothing on the running, and that you will pick a player who has to get a single bunt down. Pressure time for that player—either they pick us up or we run more. When they get it down, the entire team is pretty excited. I use this as a teachable moment, because when they are all cheering for their teammate who came through with a great bunt, there is much excitement and enthusiasm. This is the same type of energy we need in games when players get bunts down, because it means the difference between winning and losing. The team needs to pick up that player when they come back into the dugout, just as if he just hit a three-run bomb.

If you do not put something on the line, especially during bunts, players can easily get the idea that this is not important and they start to slack off. Pressure them after you have worked the mechanics of the bunt. Always challenge your team in as many game-like situations as possible.

91. ANGLE-BATTING PRACTICE

To help my players develop the ability to go the other way with the ball, one of my favorite drills is angle-batting practice. Whether we are on the field or in the cage, I like having pitches coming in from the angle. I do this to create a feel of allowing the ball to get deeper in the zone and the feel for going the other way, driving the ball with power to all fields.

We watch our players to make sure that they are not cheating the drill's purpose and changing their body's angle. We want players to stay oriented with their stance as if the ball is coming from the mound and to take a normal stride to the mound, also.

In the cages, we do a few variations of the angle-drill. Sometimes we do it underhand and sometimes we do it overhand with good speed from a coach. Other times, we might use the underhand angled toss and couple it with PowerPipes or the Total Control Balls.

One of my favorites is to set up two screens—one L-Screen at a regular mound angle and the other at an offset angle. We alternate pitches between the two locations. A coach throws from the offset angle and then the next swing is from the straight-on angle. We go back and forth for about eight swings, four from each side. The idea is that players must drive the angle-pitches back where they came from, but the pitches from the regular angle would be hit where pitched. Players seem to stay on pitches much longer and do not get so pull happy.

Another variation of this if you have enough screens is to have three screens set up—one angle screen on the 1st base side, middle (straight-up), and then angle one on the 3rd base side. If you are a right-handed hitter, you hit from the right L-screen and try to go the other way. Then, take the next pitch from the middle and hit it where it is pitched. The following pitch is from the left side, which the hitter is trying to pull and keep fair. Most players have a hard time with this, because they try to yank the ball, which means they actually get out and around the ball, causing them to pull the ball. This angle is a good way emphasize the correct way to pull the ball, which is still staying inside the ball and attacking the inside half of the ball.

92. SATO SITUATIONS

This on field hitting situation idea came from a friend of mine, Joey Sato, who is the very well-respected Head Baseball Coach at Bingham High School in Utah.

We call it Sato Situations—

Team at bat has a runner on first.

Coach pitches behind L-screen or can soft toss to hitter.

The hitter takes two swings. On the first swing, if it is a ground ball, the infield turns a double play. If it is a ball that gets through the infield, the outfield makes the throw to 3rd base, as if there is a runner trying to go from 1st to 3rd. Infielders should be in proper cut-off position or at their respective bases. The runner at 1st base does NOT run on the first ball hit.

On the second ball hit, the runner on 1st plays as if in a game and the hitter does, also. The goal of the offense is for the runner on 1st to get to 3rd base and the hitter to get to 2nd base.

Defensively, if the ball is hit on the ground, the infielders let it go into the outfield, and they are to get into position to make the play at 3rd base. Outfielders try to throw the runner out at 3rd base.

The goal of the defense is to hold the runner at 1st base from getting to 3rd or to throw out the runner at 3rd base while preventing the hitter getting to 2nd base. On routine hits to the outfield, we have started to incorporate the outfielders throwing behind the runner rounding the base at 2nd in an attempt to get an out this way. If nothing else, it prevents the other team from taking big turns, which may lead to throwing a runner out later on in the game.

This is a great way to incorporate big-time plays during a game. Turning double plays and throwing runners out when in scoring position, is a game changer and a huge rally-killer. It is a nice way to practice both, simultaneously. I hope that you find some success with this one. We only incorporate this Situation every once in a while since the outfielders are throwing so much.

93. SITUATIONS – PLAY AT THE PLATE

This is a spin on the Sato Situations and our regular Situations. We have a full defense and a hitter at the plate. What we try to create is an opportunity to work on cutting runners down at the plate. To do this, we always start with runners at 2nd and 3rd. We play the infield in and the outfield somewhat shallow, as if it was a point in the game when we have to get the out at home or the game is over. The runner at 3rd is reading down angle and breaking on contact if they see it. This is not how we play it normally, but to create pressure on our defense, we will go every time during this drill.

If this were a real game, we obviously would not go on every ground ball with the infield playing in. But to create pressure on our defense, we go every time during this drill. If there is a ground ball hit to one of our infielders, then he will come up throwing to home to try to get the runner so the catcher is able to work on making tags. Or there is the potential for a run down, also. It the rundown occurs, having a runner at 2nd base creates a situation where there are two runners going toward 3rd. This two-runner situation is often hard to defend and practice, so this will allow it to happen naturally during the Play at the Plate Drill.

If it is a base hit to the outfield, then the outfielders are throwing home to try to get the runner coming from 2nd. We send the runner from 2nd every time. Again, this is not our game strategy, but pressure is what we want for the defense. It forces them to make good throws, every time. We do not play it as a do-or-die so the infielders can cut the throw in order to get an out somewhere else during the first round.

If there is a fly ball to the outfield, we also tag at 3rd every time. The only times there are not plays at the plate are fly balls on the infield or a double, triple, or homerun.

We get the hitters through three times. This is what the rounds look like for the defense—

1. Infield in, Outfield straight up

2. Infield regular depth, Outfield straight up

3. Infield in, Outfield in, Game winners, doubles, triples, homeruns are not played out on the bases

94. FLY BALL MACHINE

As a coach, one of the best products I ever bought, without a doubt, is the ATEC Rookie Fly Ball Machine. We purchased the Major League Model that is able to shoot balls out of the outfield, if we want to. It was not cheap, but what it has to offer is worth every penny. The ability to shoot fly balls to our outfielders exactly where we want them to go is a valuable tool in developing the communication so necessary for a solid outfield. We place those in-betweeners for the outfield coming in and the infield going out. I know many coaches rely on the fungo, and so did I, but I got over the pride of doing it myself from the first time I used the Fly Ball Machine.

We use it for Twenty-One if we have a fly ball only day. We

can shoot it higher than I, or any opposing player, could ever hit the ball. We figure if our guys can catch these fly balls, we are certainly overly prepared. The machine also shoots great fly balls to your catchers for working on their fly balls. It is a piece of equipment I would use everyday to help our defense tremendously.

95. INCLINE/DECLINE TOSS

When trying to help the chronic lunger or the player who needs to develop the ability to stay behind the ball, a successful technique you can use is having them stand on a portable mound and swing from there. You can utilize the mound for soft-toss, short-toss, or live in cages. We have done all three with certain hitters. You can make something that is angled to give you the incline or decline you need for the drill, but since we have portable mounds to use in the winter, we just use those. Something smaller would be a little nicer, but the mounds work fine.

The idea is, if you have a player who likes to take his weight forward and lunge toward the ball, use the mound and have him work uphill. The incline does not allow the hitter to go and get the ball. It provides a little resistance and it feels totally awkward if he tries to go out and get the ball. The drill forces the hitter to stay back. We like to use the combo of side-toss, underhand short-toss, and finish with live pitching with the hitter. There are days we use this drill with everyone, but I like to use it with those certain hitters who might be leaking out on their front side.

The downhill angle with the portable mound is great for any hitter to develop the idea of really loading up the backside and staying behind the ball. If we do these drills with all players, we usually alternate the two angles of the mounds. One day, we do the uphill angle and the next, the downhill angle. This drill can be coupled with any overweight or underweight bats you choose. Adding a new stimulus makes it a completely different drill.

96. CURVE-FASTBALL-CURVE

I already mentioned that during our winning streak, we rarely hit on the field. Something else we do differently than others is not throwing players two fastballs in a row during their live rounds of batting practice. I strive to create practices that simulate game-like situations. To me, it never made much sense having a player get in the cage for his live round with a coach and then have him wail away at fastball, after fastball. Some teams do rounds of five, others up to ten swings. When will you ever see that many fastballs in a row? It is not preparing hitters for their game at-bats. If you are lucky, maybe you see two or three fastballs in a row.

What we do is just alternate from fastball to off-speed. I think this helps players stay balanced and also learn what it takes to adjust their swing between two different pitches. I like this approach much better than the traditional type of BP. Your players will see about the same number of fastballs and curves throughout the year. Most kids can hit a fastball well, but struggle with off-speed. This method is a way of working on strengths and weaknesses all in the same round of batting practice.

97. VIDEOTAPING HITTERS

Most teams do not have huge budgets to afford expensive video analysis equipment to record and break down a hitter's swing. What many coaches do have is an iPad, iPhone, or smart phone. We have used an app called Coach's Eye that is easy to use and works well. At $5, it is well-worth the investment. It lets you see the swing in slow motion and allows you to make marks on the screen.

During one of the first practices, we usually videotape all players in the cages and then review them as a staff that night. We critique them, writing some points down to go over with each hitter the next day during stations. We show each hitter a few of his swings and tell him what we think can be improved as we move forward.

Our schedule for videotaping everyone was early in the season, halfway point, and right before the post-season. We also video record players during games if we thought it would be helpful. We just do not want players to start to overanalyze their swings. A good balance is what we are trying to create. If a player is in a slump and we want him to see something, we use the videotape as a demonstration tool. I even use to it to show players their swings just to prove to them that their swing is mechanically sound, but their mental approach is what really needs work.

Visit www.1pitchwarrior.com/free
for the BONUS *1-Pitch Warrior*
9 "Innings" of Free *1PW* Training Resources!

NOTES:

NOTES:

NOTES:

OTHER CHARTING

The charts we keep for data measurement are always done by the players, but the next few charts are the only ones that either I, or our coaches, do. These are charts that we either use during games, when we are scouting a team we might see in the post-season, or if we are watching games at the state tournament. I once had a coach in college who would not keep track of anything. His philosophy was, if we took care of ourselves, we would win. In part I subscribe to that theory, but I also think the more information you have as a coach, you will make better decisions during the game, setting up a good practice to prepare a team, and determining what you might expect from an upcoming opponent.

98. SPRAY CHART

The only chart I have ever done during a game is the spray chart. This is obviously a homemade job, but it works for me. We have accumulated a stack of folders about two feet high about all the teams we have ever played against. Each folder represents a team we have played before and we keep all the information on that team in that folder. That way, if we play them again in the season or the next year, it is easy and convenient to find it. We pull out the spray charts and get out the kids in the line-up. Any graduated seniors are thrown away and any new players get a new spray chart sheet. Staying organized is a must if you are going to keep these types of data on a team.

The things I mark down on this sheet are—

1. Where the player is hitting the ball and if it was a groundball, fly ball, line-drive, and what type of hit it was (single, double, triple, or homerun). This allows us to position our team

defensively against hitters when we learn their tendencies. Some conference players have over twenty-eight at-bats against us and we know exactly where they are going to hit the ball before they even take a swing.

2. I mark down what type of pitch it is and if it is a swinging strike or a thrown strike. I look for patterns in the hitters. Do they always take the first pitch? Are they aggressive in the count? With what pitch are we getting them out?

3. In the record column, I also record their batting average against us. The Iowa High School Athletic Association requires teams to update stats throughout the season so you know how opposing players are hitting, which can be deceiving one way or the other. A player might be hitting .400 this season, but against us in the past, it may have only been one for ten. Or vice versa, a player might be struggling this season but had great success against us in the past. I like to mesh the two when making decisions during the game about perhaps pitching around a kid or intentionally walking a player to get to a weaker hitter.

4. The only other thing I do on the chart is add notes about the player. I might make a note that the hitter is fast, likes to steal, hits for power, drag bunts, sacrifices, or what his out pitch is. Anything that may help me next year is always helpful, because I cannot expect to remember every player on every team or his tendencies, so the spray chart becomes a valuable tool for me as a coach.

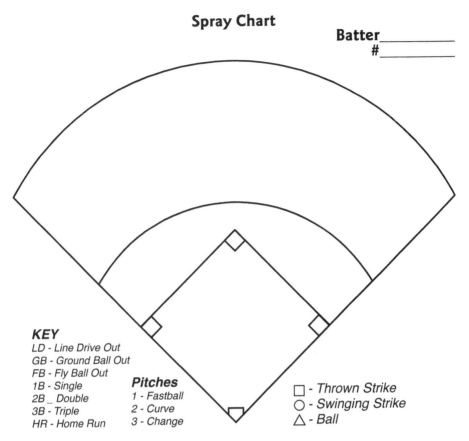

Spray Chart

Batter_____
#_____

KEY
LD - Line Drive Out
GB - Ground Ball Out
FB - Fly Ball Out
1B - Single
2B _ Double
3B - Triple
HR - Home Run

Pitches
1 - Fastball
2 - Curve
3 - Change

□ - Thrown Strike
○ - Swinging Strike
△ - Ball

AB	PITCHES	OUTCOME	RECORD	AB	PITCHES	OUTCOME	RECORD
1				16			
2				17			
3				18			
4				19			
5				20			
6				21			
7				22			
8				23			
9				24			
10				25			
11				26			
12				27			
13				28			
14				29			
15				30			

99. PITCHER'S TENDENCIES CHART

There are two things we look to collect from opposing pitchers:

1. What pitches are they throwing and in what counts?

2. What are their tendencies when runners are on?

When our hitters are up to bat, someone is charting pitchers so that we are able to learn what counts the pitcher is throwing fastball, and also, when they are using the off-speed pitch. I try to keep the chart simple and easy to read so that its meaning does not get lost in translation. I look at it from time to time during a game and also expect our hitters to do the same.

	STRIKE 0	STRIKE 1	STRIKE 3
BALL 0			
BALL 1			
BALL 2			
BALL 3			

We put an X for a fastball and an O for off-speed. If you look in the 3-1 box and see a bunch of Os, then you know the pitcher pitches backwards. It is a quick visual for hitters and can give them a better idea of what to look for on first pitch or later in an at-bat.

On the next chart, we also mark off a pitcher's tendencies about what he is doing with a runner on 1st or a lead runner at 2nd. Every new chance to pitch is a sequence. The player doing the chart is circling either H or P. If the pitcher pitches home, we mark home, how many looks he gave, and then move to the next sequence. Again, it is not rocket science to fill out the chart. At times, we have one player marking if the pitcher goes to home or

PITCHER: _____ # _____ THROWS - L R TEAM: _____

Sequence	Home/Pick	Looks	Sequence	Home/Pick	Looks
1	H P	0 1 2 3 4	1	H P	0 1 2 3 4
2	H P	0 1 2 3 4	2	H P	0 1 2 3 4
3	H P	0 1 2 3 4	3	H P	0 1 2 3 4
4	H P	0 1 2 3 4	4	H P	0 1 2 3 4
5	H P	0 1 2 3 4	5	H P	0 1 2 3 4
6	H P	0 1 2 3 4	6	H P	0 1 2 3 4
7	H P	0 1 2 3 4	7	H P	0 1 2 3 4
8	H P	0 1 2 3 4	8	H P	0 1 2 3 4
9	H P	0 1 2 3 4	9	H P	0 1 2 3 4
10	H P	0 1 2 3 4	10	H P	0 1 2 3 4
11	H P	0 1 2 3 4	11	H P	0 1 2 3 4
12	H P	0 1 2 3 4	12	H P	0 1 2 3 4
13	H P	0 1 2 3 4	13	H P	0 1 2 3 4
14	H P	0 1 2 3 4	14	H P	0 1 2 3 4
15	H P	0 1 2 3 4	15	H P	0 1 2 3 4
16	H P	0 1 2 3 4	16	H P	0 1 2 3 4
17	H P	0 1 2 3 4	17	H P	0 1 2 3 4
18	H P	0 1 2 3 4	18	H P	0 1 2 3 4
19	H P	0 1 2 3 4	19	H P	0 1 2 3 4
20	H P	0 1 2 3 4	20	H P	0 1 2 3 4
21	H P	0 1 2 3 4	21	H P	0 1 2 3 4
22	H P	0 1 2 3 4	22	H P	0 1 2 3 4
23	H P	0 1 2 3 4	23	H P	0 1 2 3 4
24	H P	0 1 2 3 4	24	H P	0 1 2 3 4
25	H P	0 1 2 3 4	25	H P	0 1 2 3 4
12	H P	0 1 2 3 4	26	H P	0 1 2 3 4
27	H P	0 1 2 3 4	27	H P	0 1 2 3 4
28	H P	0 1 2 3 4	28	H P	0 1 2 3 4
29	H P	0 1 2 3 4	29	H P	0 1 2 3 4
30	H P	0 1 2 3 4	30	H P	0 1 2 3 4
31	H P	0 1 2 3 4	31	H P	0 1 2 3 4
32	H P	0 1 2 3 4	32	H P	0 1 2 3 4
33	H P	0 1 2 3 4	33	H P	0 1 2 3 4
34	H P	0 1 2 3 4	34	H P	0 1 2 3 4
35	H P	0 1 2 3 4	35	H P	0 1 2 3 4
36	H P	0 1 2 3 4	36	H P	0 1 2 3 4

MAX HOLDS:_____
MAX LOOKS:_____

IF RUNNERS ARE AT 1ST AND 2ND, ONLY CHART FOR A RUNNER AT 2ND

1st and another counting looks. We look for a few things here. Does the pitcher ever pick twice in a row? What is the maximum number of looks he has given at 1st? At 2nd? If we know that he never picks twice in a row to 2nd and that his max looks to 2nd is two, what better advantage can a base stealer have than knowing this? Once the game is over, this info is going into the opposing team's folder and will be used for next year.

100. SCOUTING CHART

In the past, as I scouted teams that we were playing in the post-season, I always had a ton of information I gathered, but it was never all in one spot. It created confusion, was not organized, and I could not access the information I needed. I created this chart for a more compact and easier to read version of all the other things I had.

Using the chart I collect valuable information that helps in preparing a solid game plan to attack the other team. As you can see, knowing the catcher's pop time from home to 2nd is going to let us know who can steal on our team and who cannot. Simple math will tell us whom we can send and who is right on the bubble. This way there is no guessing game. The only time we take a calculated risk is with those players who might be right on the verge. Taking the average on the catcher's pop times, added to the pitcher's time to home, gives us the magic number our players have to beat to 2nd. Remember, we have already tested our players with their own steal average to 2nd. This is something worth testing again after the regular season is over. Some players could have lost a step or possibly gained one, too. Best to have accurate information.

During the team's pre-game, I like to take a look at the outfielder's arms and will rate each one on a scale of 1-10 at the bottom of

Opposing Pitcher Holding Runners Chart

OPPONENT:

Pitcher:

Catcher Pop Time:

Bunt Defense:

Pitchers Delivery Time:

At 1st | At 2nd | 1st/3rd Defense:

Runners @ 1st — Slide Step | Leg Kick — Max Look | Looks

Runners @ 2nd — Slide Step | Leg Kick — Max Look | Look

Pitch Sequence by Batter

	1	2	3	4	5	6	7	8	9
1									
2									
3									
4									
5									
6									
7									
8									
9									

MPH by Inning

	1	2	3	4	5	6	7	8	9
Fastball	Fastball	Fastball	Fastball	Fastball	Fastball	Fastball	Fastball	Fastball	Fastball
Curve	Curve	Curve	Curve	Curve	Curve	Curve	Curve	Curve	Curve
Change	Change	Change	Change	Change	Change	Change	Change	Change	Change

OF ARM STRENGTH SIGNS	LF =	C =	RF =

the page, one being terrible and ten being amazing. Information like this is certainly useful when attempting to extend singles to doubles and doubles to triple and when scoring runners for our base coaches.

I also count looks to each base getting an idea if the pitcher is always slide step or only in certain counts or with certain types of runners. We give our players this information and then try to recreate at practices leading up to the game.

I also have a spot to make notes on anything special they do with bunt coverage and 1st and 3rd defense. Some teams have different strategies with those, but if I get a good read that they do not take chances with runners at 1st and 3rd, then I might steal a player who normally I would not. If I know they like to try to get the stealing runner during 1st and 3rd situations, then I will be more apt to have the runner try to score from 3rd. Also, knowing where their players go during bunt situations helps us for possibly trying to create havoc with double steals, fake bunt steals, or just bunting the ball in a spot that will make it tougher on the defense to get an out.

I record the sequence to each hitter much like I do on the Spray Chart. At the same time, I am watching the radar gun to see the top speed of each pitch and record that at the bottom of the chart. I do this each inning and watch for the pitcher's stamina. Does he start off strong but his velocity drops quickly after the second inning? What is his speed differential in pitches? These are things we can recreate at practice with our pitching machine throwing curveballs and our coaches throwing the same speed as his fastball with some simple proportional calculations.

$$\frac{Pitcher's\ MPH}{60.5\ Feet} \times \frac{Coach's\ MPH}{Distance\ coach\ should\ be\ from\ home}$$

In order for this to work, you need to have a radar gun to clock your coach who is throwing. Cross multiply 60.5 by your coach's MPH, then divide by how fast the pitcher you expect to face is throwing, and you will know exactly from where to have your coach throw. For example, if the pitcher you scout, and are likely to face, is throwing 82 MPH and your coach throws 60 MPH, things would look like this:

$$\frac{82\ MPH}{60.5\ Feet} \times \frac{60\ MPH}{Distance\ from\ home\ (X)}$$

$$60\ x\ 60.5 = 82\ X$$

$$3630 = 82\ X$$

$$\frac{3630}{82} = X$$

$$44.3\ feet\ from\ home = X$$

Too many times we guess, assume, or just think it is good enough, but the best teams will take the time necessary to commit to excellence in all aspects of the game.

101. THE MOTION OFFENSE

One thing I know is that great coaches and programs adapt philosophies and strategies to fit their personnel. You cannot plan on hitting a 3-run bomb every night, when your line-up has no power. You cannot plan to steal bases and create havoc, when you have no speed. Hopefully, you have a little of both, but sometimes, you have only one or the other. In 2010, 2011, and 2012, we were lucky enough to have a lot of power putting us in the top five in homeruns each year, in all classes in the state. We hit 51 homeruns in 2010, which was the first in the state, 54 in 2011 which was second in the state, and 31 in the 2012 (post BBCOR) campaign, which was fifth in the state. We also had a few players with some speed on the bases, so we could beat you with our legs and hit for power, too—certainly a nice combination to have.

Going into the 2013 season, the power graduated and with the introduction of the new bats, homeruns were at an all-time low. The one thing we did have in our favor was a team that was extremely fast. In fact, it was the fastest I have ever been associated with. Coach Fitzpatrick and I knew that coming up with a game plan that would allow our biggest strength to shine through would be critical to our success. What we came up with was the Motion Offense. Its intent was to create havoc and utter chaos on the base paths. We created an outline of all the things we thought would be needed to score runs.

Motion Offense Outline

Develop a mindset to obtain an extra 90ft. at every opportunity.

- **Base running** – is a mindset; every pitch is an opportunity to take a bag

- **Make the ball in the dirt** – when the catcher flips his glove, you go (practice this with catcher)

- If we get to 2nd before the OF has the ball, we go every time

4-hole hitting – let the ball travel

- Drill – Play groundball BP during situations

- Situations – 1 to 2 rounds must be on the ground, not a fly ball hitting team, make the other team make the tough play

1st to 3rd

- Confident – if you are at 1st you are going to 3rd

- Set the tone – gives your team an image

- Put pressure on the other team

- Steal and bunt – trying to get to 3rd

- Know where your outfielders are at every base

- Practice – pick up your base coach (coach-bag-coach)

1st and 3rd Steals

- Every time, automatic

- 2 outs and trying to get 1 run across, we break early and get in a run down, runner from 3rd goes when 1st baseman turns his shoulders to throw

- 1 or no outs, we straight steal and stop ¾ of the way to get in a run down

- Runner at 3rd goes once the ball has been released to 2nd, cannot creep too far down the line

- Fake squeeze (coach and dugout sell the squeeze), with steal at 1st – First pitch

- Safety Steal Squeeze – if the runner from 3rd does go home, the runner at 1st is trying to get to 3rd

Stealing Home

- Identify the pitcher's pattern – is he checking you?

- Identify the catcher's pattern – what is his throw back to the pitcher like?

- Where is the 3rd basemen?

- Lefty – is a better chance

- Can we go in between the throw back to the pitcher?

Early break 1st and 3rd

- Right before the pitcher comes set, you are taking 2nd base until stopped. The guy at 3rd starts running as soon as the 1st basemen gets it and his momentum goes to 2nd

- Difficult to defend

- Trying to extend a lead

Stealing

- It is going to take about 1.3 sec from pitcher to catcher, 2.2 sec from catcher to 2nd, and .2 sec for the tag. 1.3 + 2.2 + 0.2 = 3.7

- Super aggressive with 2 outs – with 2 outs get to 2nd as soon as possible because if you are at 1st you need hits to score

- Players need to feel comfortable making aggressive mistakes

- 2 outs scoring from 2nd every time

- Runners at 1st and 2nd – fake bunt steal, creating extra things for the defense to defend, next pitch could be the double squeeze, continue to put pressure on the defense to make plays

- Automatic Steals – Runner at 2nd, 2-2 count, 1 or 2 outs, 3-1 count runner, at 1st

- Curveball counts – 0-2/1-2 counts

Bunting

- If you cannot bunt, you will not play

- Put the pressure on the D by forcing them to make plays

- 1st and 3rd, 0 outs, safety squeeze

- 1st and 3rd fake squeeze SB

- Guy at 3rd fake breaks, guy at 1st steals 2nd

- With runner at 1st, steal or fake steal to get 2nd baseman to cover and push bunt to that side to create havoc for the right side of the infield

Down Angle

- Read down angle out of pitcher's hand

- In practice, every time we see down angle we must go, no exceptions

- Work on reads during base running sessions, as well

- Set up a screen between pitcher and catcher so base runners are forced to read early instead of keying on catcher

Double Squeeze

- Fast runner at 2nd is touching 3rd – bunt goes down 3rd

- Slow runner at 2nd is cutting corner – bunt goes down 1st

Slash

- Use when opposing team is expecting a bunt for sure, especially when we have already bunted a few times or the current batter has laid a bunt down before in the game

- Square around early, see the top half of the ball

- Work this in situations on a daily basis/situations

Runner at 3rd

- Walk, hitter busts it to 1st and never stops going straight to 2nd, create chaos, with 2 outs or to extend a lead

- Runner at 3rd is waiting for the distraction or throw, if there is a throw to the middle he is going home, no throw then stays at 3rd with runners at 2nd and 3rd

- If we have runners at 2nd and 3rd then the next hitters should be ready to squeeze/double squeeze

Delay Steal

- If middle is not pinching in between pitches, then at some point during the game, we will take an extra 90 feet

Dugout

- Expectations are that everyone knows the pitcher's timing

- Early in the game we are trying to get reads and times on new pitchers

- Find the pattern – either time-wise or number of looks, all pitchers have patterns, we just have to find it and take a calculated risk

- Pick up coach for number of max looks up to that point in the game, if he gets to that point, then go!

- During squeeze, they can be yelling GO, GO, GO, create adversity for the other team

Automatic Steals

- 3-1 counts, no sign needed

- 1-2 counts, off-speed counts we can get more time to get to the next base, plus a more difficult pitch to handle

Bench

- Anyone with speed needs to be ready to pinch run at any point in the game with the intent to steal

- Every time we hit, specified runners will go either to foul pole or run behind the dugout to stay loose

- Stay in the game, be a student of the game

2 Outs/2 Strikes

- Looking for great jumps off the bat

- As soon as you see the swing begin you are going, no questions asked

Our plan of attack worked well for us. We stole 278 bases, which was second in the state and fifth best all-time in the state record books. In addition, we had a player break the state record for steals. With a team that only hit nine homeruns on the year,

Justin Dehmer

we were able to tap into creating pressure on the other team with our motion offense and score over 400 runs for the fourth year in a row. I hope you are able to incorporate some of these techniques and strategies into your program and make the most of the speed you have.

Visit www.store.1pitchwarrior.com
Order your copy of the *1-Pitch Warrior* DVD System to have all the resources at your finger tips to start creating *1PW*s in your program.

NOTES:

NOTES:

NOTES:

FINAL THOUGHTS

As you can see, there are many facets of a *1-Pitch Warrior*. I hope that these 101 Tools have given you insight into our program and the things we were doing while our winning streak was alive. The methods we used to prepare, both physically and mentally, were certainly keys for us in winning back-to-back-to-back state titles. You are now Equipped for Excellence. After reading this book, you have the knowledge to create solid practices, the strategies to teach the mental game to your players, and the ability to implement strategies that are process-based and deliver big results.

Remember, you can have all the knowledge in the world, but if you do not put that knowledge to use, then you are no better off than the coach who knows nothing about the game. Knowledge without action gets you nothing, so take action! Use the things you have learned to make a difference in your program. Stay focused on the process, win pitches in the present, and dominate your days as a *1-Pitch Warrior*!

SELECT BIBLIOGRAPY

Listed here are writings that have served as inspirations for my coaching and this book.

Cain, Brian. The Mental Conditioning Manual—Your Blueprint for Excellence, Revised 2nd Edition, 2013

Cain, Brian. So What, Next Pitch!—How to Play Your Best, When it Means to Most, 2012

Cain, Brian. Toilets, Bricks, Fish Hooks and PRIDE—The Peak Performance Toolbox Exposed, Revised 3rd Edition, 2012

ABOUT THE AUTHOR

Justin Dehmer's playing career started in Arizona at Shadow Mountain High School and continued into college with three different stops, including Central Arizona, where he was able to play in a JUCO World Series and become an Academic All-American. From there, Dehmer played at Kansas State University and Grand Canyon University. Once in Iowa, Dehmer jumped right into the coaching ranks as the Assistant Varsity Coach at Earlham High School for two years and then as the Head Coach for two more years before landing the job at Martensdale-St. Marys for five more years. He boasts an impressive 203-48 (.829) winning record and was selected as Coach of the Year in 2010, 2011, and 2012. His team was nationally recognized for its 88-game winning streak, which is the 2nd best ever in high school baseball. After winning back-to-back-to-back State Championships in 2010 (43-0), 2011 (44-0), 2012 (40-5), Coach Dehmer left coaching high school baseball to invest time in what means more to him than any championship—his family. He continues to teach high school math at Southeast Polk and resides in Norwalk, Iowa with his two children, Grace, 7 and son Gavin, 6. He continues to stay close to the game as a clinic speaker, writing books/articles for baseball publications, and consulting for both high school and college programs about the mental game and planning for excellence with the *1-Pitch Warrior* System.

NOTES:

www.1pitchwarrior.com

NOTES:

NOTES:

NOTES:

I-PITCH WARRIOR SYSTEM WILL

- Give you the Team Process Index Scoring System
- Teach you how to play 1-Pitch-at-a-Time
- Hand you the keys to unlock your potential
- Teach you toughness between the lines
- Provide you a step-by-step development plan

Order NOW Online
www.1PitchWarrior.com

www.twitter.com/1PitchWarrior

www.facebook.com/1PitchWarrior

1-PITCH WARRIOR SYSTEM v2.0

- 45-MINUTE HITTING VIDEO
- 90 *IPW* PRESENTATION VIDEO
- PITCHING PROCESS AUDIO
- *IPW* AUDIO
- ANATOMY OF A WINNING STREAK AUDIO
- INTERVIEW WITH BRIAN CAIN
- MENTAL TOUGHNESS AUDIOS
- *IPW* DOCUMENTS AND FILES

A $200+ VALUE FOR ONLY $99
GO TO www.1PitchWarrior.com
TO ORDER

1-PITCH WARRIOR
MENTALITY TRAINING

Have Justin work directly with your team and coaches to customize and fine tune your own *1-Pitch Warrior* Training Program

Learn the ABCs of a *1-Pitch Warrior*

To play your best you must be able to Act Big, Breathe Big, and Commit Big! In my training sessions, I break down these ideas into clear-cut concepts and action steps both players and coaches can use to improve the mental game, the  way to focus on the present moment, and the process to be competitive, night in and night out. We used these skills for our 88-game winning streak and back-to-back-to-back state titles. You can learn them, too.

Act Big—We discuss the concept that feelings are not facts and how time management is so crucial to achieve greatness. Our thoughts determine what we want but our actions determine what we get.

Breathe Big—Learn how to slow down the game and stay in control of emotions. I will train your players how to respond to the highs and lows of a game, season, and career by focusing on the present moment, taking things 1-Pitch-at-a-Time.

Commit Big—Knowledge minus action gets you nothing— learning everything but failing to apply the training is all for naught. Build team chemistry and unity and overcome fears through fun challenges.

1-PITCH WARRIOR Training Sessions with Players and Staff Include:

- A Step-by-Step Overview and Instruction of the *1-Pitch Warrior* Process-Based Measurement System covering Quality-At Bats, B.A.S.E.2., Quality Innings, A3P, S.T.R.1.K.E., and Team Process Index.

- Ways to Implement the Mental Game in Practice Sessions and a Look at a Master Practice Schedule

- A Q&A with Coaches

- Consultation on What to Change or How to Keep Moving Forward

- The *1-Pitch Warrior* System DVD

- Electronic Forms of the Spreadsheets, Word, and pdf Documents to Track Performances and Inform Players and Parents of Key Program Initiatives and Requirements, and more

- 20-Minute Follow-Up Consultations Every Week

FOR MORE DETAILS
ON THESE TRAINING SESSIONS, GO TO
WWW.1PITCHWARRIOR.COM

"The *1-Pitch Warrior* seminar is one of the best things our athletic department has done for our student-athletes and coaches in the 11 years that I have been at NIACC. Justin is an amazing motivator and he has had an immeasurable impact on our student-athletes lives, on and off the field."

- Tyler Sisco
Head Softball Coach
North Iowa Area Community College

HOW CAN YOU BECOME A TRUE
MASTER OF THE MENTAL GAME?

Brian Cain offers a range of training
materials to get you or your team to the top of
your game. Available at www.BrianCain.com

MASTERS OF THE MENTAL GAME SERIES BOOKS

The Daily Dominator: **Perform Your Best Today. Every Day!** You get 366 Daily Mental Conditioning lessons to help you start your day down the path to excellence. Investing time each day with Cain is your best way to become your best self.	
The Mental Conditioning Manual: **Your Blueprint For Excellence** This is the exact system Cain uses to build champions and masters of the mental game and has helped produce NCAA and High School, champions, MMA world champions, and more.	
So What, Next Pitch: **How To Play Your Best When It Means The Most** A compilation of interviews with top coaches and players where Cain teaches you their systems and tricks. Learn from the insights of these masters of the mental game.	
Toilets Bricks Fish Hooks and PRIDE: **The Peak Performance Toolbox EXPOSED** Go inside the most successful programs in the country that use Cain's Peak Performance System. Use this book to unlock your potential and learn to play your best when it means the most.	
Champions Tell All: **Inexpensive Experience From The World's Best** Cain provides you with all access to some of the World's greatest performers. Learn from mixed martial arts world champions and college All-Americans about mental toughness.	

"Cain has tapped into the mental side of baseball and softball performance like no one else. He is the industry leader. Everyone else is playing catch up."

—*Jim Schlossnagle*
Head Baseball Coach
Texas Christian University
2010 NCAA National Coach of The Year
2013 Team USA Baseball Collegiate National Team Field Manager

www.BrianCain.com

MENTAL CONDITIONING & PEAK PERFORMANCE TRAINING TOOLS

### Brian Cain's 4RIP3 Softball ### Mental Conditioning Program This is the best mental conditioning program ever created for softball coaches and players. In these 10 audios, Cain takes you through his signature 4RIP3 System used by all of the top collegiate programs in the country. You get 3 cds and a 300 page manual that takes you to the next level of toughness.	
### The Peak Performance System: (P.R.I.D.E.) ### Personal Responsibility In Daily Excellence This big, video-based training program is Cain's signature training program for coaches, athletes and teams. It will take you step by step to the top of the performance mountain.	
### Diamond Domination Training This training program is being used by 11 teams in the NCAA top 25 in college baseball and 8 of the top 25 in college softball. It will help you and your team to unlock your potential and play the best baseball and softball of your life.	
### The Peak Performance Boot Camp This introductory program will give you the tools, power, and mental toughness you need to be prepared for every game, every play, and every minute. Learn techniques to get the absolute best chance of maximizing your potential and getting the most out of your ability.	

"Cain's programs will not only help you on the field, it will help you in life."

–Nate Yeskie
Assistant Baseball Coach, Oregon State University

"Brian Cain will give you and your team a system for playing at your best when it means the most."

Todd Whitting
Head Baseball Coach, University of Houston

"Brian Cain is the best mental game coach I have seen in all of my clinics/conventions I have attended over the years. OUTSTANDING!!!"

Lonni Alemeda,
Head Softball Coach, Florida State University

"Cain's books will give you a formula for success between the ears."

Bob Tewksbury,
Sport Psychology Consultant, Boston Red Sox

www.BrianCain.com

CONNECT WITH CAIN
THROUGH SOCIAL MEDIA
YOUR LINK TO DOING A LITTLE A LOT, NOT A LOT A LITTLE

 www.twitter.com/briancainpeak

 www.facebook.com/briancainpeak

 www.linkedin.com/briancainpeak

 www.youtube.com/wwwbriancaincom

 www.briancain.com/itunes

SIGN UP FOR THE
PEAK PERFORMANCE NEWSLETTER

Cain's newsletter is full of information to help you unlock your potential and perform at your best when it means the most. Subscribe for free and get a bonus audio training.

www.BrianCain.com/newsletter

DOMINATE
THE DAY!!!

NOTES:

NOTES: